Completely Satisfied

Hank Marquis

Published by MarquisPrècis, 2023.

Table of Contents

Praise for *Completely Satisfied*

"With the release of his new book Completely Satisfied, Hank has provided a detailed roadmap for IT leaders that is comprehensive, timely, and relevant. It's packed with decades of know-how and actionable guidance critical to moving from an issue-driven, reactive orientation to one that is proactive and entirely focused on delivering value to those that consume IT products and services. Do yourself a favor and rip this book apart! Take the time to consider Hank's recommendation and get started on your satisfaction journey – you won't be sorry."

Kenneth Gonzalez, IT industry advisor & former Gartner Analyst

"Hank Marquis perfectly captures the subtle yet profound shift in thinking IT leaders need to make to deliver IT products and services that improve digital employee experience."

Larry Cooper, Chief Strategy Officer, The Hive Professional Network

"Completely Satisfied is a welcome addition to the limited number of books about capturing and improving digital employee experience. Wherever you are in your IT satisfaction improvement journey, it has something to offer. IT satisfaction improvement is a journey, and Completely Satisfied guides you step by step."

Mark Smalley, lead editor ITIL® 4 High-velocity IT and content editor XLA® Pocketbook.

"Stunning insights into the subject and all conveyed with a conversational style that has just carried me along."

Bhupinder D'Mahi, Investor, Entrepreneur, Independent Researcher

Completely Satisfied

How to Nail IT Satisfaction

for Employee Experience,

Productivity & Profits

DISCLAIMER: I'm an active C-level information technology leadership advisor, but I'm not *your* advisor, and buying this book doesn't create a client relationship between us, so check with your advisors before taking any drastic actions. The Satisfaction Stories in this book are "reality fiction" — condensed, realistic, and illustrative examples of common IT problems and subsequent solutions based on my IT practitioner, educator, and consultant career working with thousands of individuals at hundreds of firms spanning decades.

Visit www.hankmarquis.com for free templates and expanded content.

ACKNOWLEDGEMENTS

Stephen Covey said, "Interdependence is a higher value than independence."

This book and its approach are products of nearly two decades of experimentation and learning that started with my doctoral program at the dawn of the 21st century. I discovered that even the simplest-looking topics are far from simple — IT satisfaction is a great example.

I thank researchers of the 1970s, '80s, and '90s who built on the work of earlier pioneers to develop human satisfaction and experience psychographics (how people think and act) and psychometrics (measuring psychographics), as well as thought leaders of today pushing the boundaries of IT digital employee experience and connecting employee experience to business agility and corporate profits.

Covey's phrase perfectly captures the sentiment of Completely Satisfied. It inspired me to write this book. I promise you'll find my approaches useful as you co-create better digital employee experiences with your customers and users.

Start where you are right now. Share with your team as you learn. Don't wait, fixated on an idealized, illusional, and unachievable end state. IT satisfaction improvement is a journey, and Completely Satisfied guides you step by step.

I have found IT satisfaction a constant struggle for many because you can't buy, outsource, or install it — and no tool will solve your IT satisfaction problem. You have to shift your perspective and learn to lead differently.

As you gain new skills, you'll find IT satisfaction a changing target. Covey also said, "The better you get, the very nature of the challenge changes, just like skiing, playing golf, tennis, or any sport does." Digital employee experience is no exception, and I welcome you to the sport of modern IT leadership!

— Hank Marquis

www.hankmarquis.com

hank@hankmarquis.com

www.linkedin.com/in/hankmarquis

July 15, 2023

PROLOGUE

You've got a neat digital workplace solution, but employees don't like it. Your IT operational metrics say they're happy, but they say they're not. Productivity and profit are down.

You think this is a training or Human Resource problem at first. You believe that if employees aren't satisfied or productive with the IT solutions you provide, it has to be because they're untrained, or you need to give them the right technology.

But if that were true, additional IT spending would result in a better digital employee experience — higher satisfaction, increased employee productivity, and more profits. Yet you're spending more on IT than ever, and IT satisfaction is at an all-time low.

YOU'VE GOT AN

IT SATISFACTION

PROBLEM.

I'VE GOT A

SIMPLE 10-STEP

SOLUTION.

INTRODUCTION

I frequently speak with IT leaders. When I ask about IT satisfaction, I always hear, "Yeah, we're doing that already."

I get it. IT satisfaction is as unpopular as it is familiar. You might even think there is little to learn about IT satisfaction by now, but you'd be wrong. While most of us know what IT satisfaction is, only a few know how to deliver it.

How we equip our digital employees with technology continues to morph and expand. Today's remote and hybrid digital workplace solutions include:

- Dozens of SaaS and software applications.
- Half a dozen meeting and conference options.
- Multiple collaboration tools.
- Perhaps an AI chatbot.

Most IT leaders ask employees how much they like this technology and regularly check if they would recommend IT to a friend or are satisfied with IT. So, you can understand why many IT and business leaders think they've already handled digital employee experience (aka DEX) satisfaction.

Then why do I talk about a situation already dealt with? Why write a book on leading with IT satisfaction? Why would anyone want to read a book on it?

There are two main reasons for this book. First, IT satisfaction levels appear to be at an all-time low, partly due to the increasing complexity I just mentioned! Second, there's no longer a line between IT and business. Today, every dollar of profit and loss depends on the digital employee experience we deliver.

> "Start with the customer experience and work backward to the technology."
>
> — *Steve Jobs*

Yet most of us must do more to improve our DEX. In other words, if your digital employees are unhappy, the tech you've implemented isn't making them successful. They need to achieve their desired business results, and you can help them.

Leading with satisfaction isn't your task; it's your philosophy.

It's deliberately discovering what employees at the other end of your IT solutions (users) and their leadership (customers) care most about and making that experience the core of your leadership.

It's looking at everything you do for ways to improve the experience of your employees and those who use the IT solutions you deliver, whatever those solutions may be.

Ask yourself, "Why is this done this way? Can we do it better? Do we need to do it better?" You have to be fundamentally skeptical and question everything.

Want higher employee productivity? Get a better understanding of how to measure employee experience authentically. Want to up satisfaction? Ask digital employees what they dislike most about IT. Want to boost profits? Find out what makes employees the most engaged and productive.

We must ensure that satisfaction is at the heart of every IT solution, service, and product we build or deliver and every business function we support. It should be the starting point of every conversation we have.

We must consider IT a service, not a technology to achieve this. We must focus on designing experiences that are simple, intuitive, and engaging. We must think about how our solutions make our employees feel and how they can help them succeed.

Failing at IT satisfaction is failing to lead IT. When IT fails, our business fails.

IT satisfaction is an excellent measure of your IT performance. But throwing more money and tech at the problem isn't usually the answer when it's low. Counterintuitively, most of the time, it just worsens employee experience, and satisfaction drops even more.

Think of it this way. If an employee struggles to find a client record, it's not their fault. It's probably because the process is complicated and takes too long, using too many different tools. You can't blame users. However, you can blame it on needing more focus on satisfaction with digital experience.

This problem is so pervasive that it even has a name, "digital friction." It affects everyone — us in IT, internal employees, and external customers and partners. It's like pedaling a bike into a headwind, taking more effort to go anywhere. It's an IT experience killer and a productivity sinkhole.

> "We cannot solve our problems with the same thinking we used when we created them."
>
> *— Albert Einstein*

Think you don't have to worry about digital friction? Think again! Recent surveys show that it wastes up to 34% of employee time. Take a moment to consider how this impacts your business — not only in terms of employee turnover and low engagement but also in terms of end-customer churn and lost profits.

The best IT leaders are champions for a firm's external customers.

Zeroing in on the potential impact of IT decisions on your external marketplace also subsumes your digital employees' needs.

Following is a recent example of what happens when you don't. I call these examples *Satisfaction Stories* and will use them throughout.

***

Satisfaction Story: *For Want of Leadership Focused on IT Satisfaction*

Background: The IT organization of a legal services firm decided to force an update to the next version of their desktop productivity suite. The suite's email application didn't have the same features as the previous version. IT planners didn't use those features and thought no one else did (or worse, didn't know those features existed!) Thus, IT communicated no guidance to users, and users got the new version the next time they started the email application.

Results: The forced upgrade lost thousands of client notes.

Conclusion: Affected customer contact employees were unhappy and unable to support their clients and partners. Engagement dropped. External customer satisfaction, loyalty, and profits fell.

***

When your teams work on an IT solution, start with those outside your company who buy or use your products and services. Understand how your internal employees support those marketplaces and relationships. Ensure you test every IT product and service idea against the desired outcomes and the results it creates.

Leading with satisfaction is the key to a smooth workflow for everyone.

Being satisfaction-centric improves morale and makes good business sense. Giving our digital employees IT solutions that satisfy them means they're getting desired results — they can do their job well with your IT kit!

Let's use satisfaction to our advantage and ensure we eliminate digital friction and deliver the results our employees need. Great IT satisfaction accelerates your business, putting you one move ahead of your competition.

I've called this work *satisfactioneering*, and those that practice my approach *satisfactioneers*.

But satisfaction has a satisfaction problem.

When I chat with IT and business leaders about leading with satisfaction, it usually takes a while to get on the same page regarding what satisfaction is and isn't. Some think it means monitoring operational technology, the so-called "speeds and feeds" of information technology solutions. Others think it's about asking employees now and then how much they like IT, and others think it only applies to the IT service or help desk.

Satisfaction can be tricky for logical-minded IT leaders because it's more about subjective feelings than objective technology. Leading with satisfaction requires putting people and their needs first and tech second, which can be challenging for some ITers.

Plus, satisfaction is different between IT solutions and between workgroups for the same IT solution — one workgroup's idea of satisfaction might not work for another. So far, I haven't met many in IT who said they lead with satisfaction, but those I did were winners.

The first step to optimizing digital employee satisfaction is understanding what it's not.

Satisfaction isn't a number, a survey, or a score. It's the opinion of very important people — your customers and users.

I know that idea is new to some IT leaders and their teams. But I've found that it helps to consider satisfaction as your "leadership compass" for IT. It gives you a clear idea of your "true north." It shows you what to do, for whom, and why.

That way, we're all headed in the right direction and avoiding the headaches of trying to resolve dissatisfaction. Without it, everyone loses out — including us — and nobody's happy.

> "If I had to run a company on three measures, those measures would be customer satisfaction, employee satisfaction, and cash flow."
>
> — *Jack Welch*

I've seen IT leaders following their "true north" identify improvement areas and get impressive investment returns.

But I've also seen IT leaders who didn't and watched them brush off changes to increase productivity and profits. It's a shame because if we break our old habits, we can take advantage of opportunities that could completely change the game.

IT satisfaction is like a misunderstood superpower. It will change how you think, act, and lead.

Behind this confusion are the many ways to measure satisfaction with an experience. Is there one best way to measure digital workplace satisfaction, or is any method as good as another? Can't IT products gauge satisfaction automatically? Can you be strategic about experience satisfaction, or is it tactical?

In 1980, Dr. Noriaki Kano revolutionized product management by introducing a model for customer-defined quality. It outlined five requirements for customers to have a great product experience and three types of product requirements. Businesses started using Kano's model to adjust product investments based on consumer needs.

Today, many IT organizations still rely on Kano's model to create CSAT surveys — which isn't ideal. Kano designed his model for product management. Today there are more up-to-date models to measure and improve IT satisfaction.

The next step was the concept of service satisfaction as distinct from product satisfaction. This approach became a popular marketing construct in 1988 with the publication of SERVQUAL by "Parsu" Parasuraman, Valarie Ziethaml, and Leonard Berry (PZB.)

They argued that service businesses could stand out by understanding customers' expectations and perceptions and using the gap between them to measure and improve their experience quality. Their big ideas were that quality is satisfaction over time and that there are just five determinants of service quality. They showed us that you could measure and shape satisfaction using psychometric tools.

PZB clarified that customer satisfaction was crucial but presented their concept in a marketing science journal as a basic skeleton to adapt to fit one's needs. In other words, heavy reading for marketing professors.

So, it sat for a while. And then came the one-liners.

How likely are you to recommend us to a friend or colleague?

In 2003, Fred Reichheld, then a Partner at Bain & Company, a global consultancy, created *Net Promoter Score* (NPS.) It's a "one-line" customer loyalty measure. Most of us know it from buying on the Internet. Its question is usually a variation of: "On a scale from 0-10, how likely are you to recommend us to a friend or colleague?"

NPS is non-diagnostic. That means if your score is low, you need to use another approach to know what caused it to be so. Nor do you know what "good looks like," even if you did, you couldn't unpack an NPS score into the five factors humans use to decide whether we're satisfied.

The company made it easy for me to handle my issue.

In 2010, the Corporate Executive Board created the *Customer Effort Score* (CES) when their research showed that "effort" is a crucial driver of customer loyalty.

Like NPS, CES is a "one-line survey." CES's question is usually, "To what extent do you agree with the following statement: The company made it easy for me to handle my issue."

Like NPS, CES isn't diagnostic.

However, both are valuable in identifying a dissatisfied individual, albeit in different circumstances.

Do we need yet another book on IT satisfaction?

Since IT satisfaction has been an important topic for so long, you'd think we'd all know how to deliver, measure and lead with it, right? That's what I thought when I started trying to improve IT delivery by removing digital friction. But I quickly realized that many satisfaction measures like CES and NPS don't measure user-perceived *Quality of Experience* (QoE) — the difference between IT consumer (customers and users) perception and expectation.

I found measuring satisfaction piecemeal wasn't enough — it doesn't tell us why someone might be dissatisfied, only that they are, which was very frustrating. I realized that we needed a diagnostic satisfaction solution.

I encountered many approaches and vendors discussing satisfaction, but none had a method for systematically improving it. I found no one with an answer for leading with it or delivering and improving the quality of experience in a human way based on the employee's feelings about the results they get from using the tech vs. the tech itself.

Everything I found centered on technical, operational metrics, the so-called IT "speeds and feeds."

But nowadays, it's almost impossible to separate services from products — and we rely heavily on customer satisfaction to survive.

If satisfaction diagnosis was interesting in the 1980s, we live and die by it today.

Most of us were trying to deliver satisfaction but weren't doing it correctly.

As an IT consultant and leader, I focused on improving IT by working backward from employee satisfaction and productivity.

I started using all the traditional IT satisfaction approaches and eventually realized what didn't work. Every client engagement was an opportunity to learn something new. I refined my approach after working with others who shared the same vision of how employee satisfaction and productivity can lead to better business results and higher profits. Our focus on diagnosing user satisfaction worked.

We learned how to analyze employee experience from a people-centric (*humanistic*) perspective.

Humanistic metrics measure people's satisfaction qualitatively by looking at how they feel about their IT solutions — the emotions of their achievements. Our humanistic approach showed us how to measure an employee's IT experience. We were like medical doctors reading a patient's EKG to determine heart health. We had the key to designing and delivering the perfect business experience.

Thanks to this, I had a reliable way of leading with satisfaction. After I'd diagnosed satisfaction in hundreds of cloud service providers, tech organizations, IT field service units, and corporations, I felt confident enough to share my knowledge with others. I started blogging about my approach, presented the strategy at IT industry events, and consulted for Fortune 50-1000 firms.

I created templates and tools and founded, led, and sold software and SaaS companies to automate different methods. I built a web-based AI tool to automate my new approach. I was a premier IT executive coach for a well-known global advisory company. I've been lucky to learn from supportive and skeptical IT leaders who have helped me perfect my technique over the years.

The process in this book is thoroughly researched, tested, and proven reliable to connect IT experience with technology to deliver the desired outcomes that satisfy digital employees and bring business results. That's why we needed a new book on IT satisfaction. This book is it!

- I'll show you how to understand your satisfied and dissatisfied IT customers and users by teaching you the drivers of satisfaction and dissatisfaction among workgroups.
- I'll teach you how IT satisfaction breaks down into five components so that you can perfect each one.
- I'll teach you how to design IT solutions and experiences that make employees more productive and help your business make more money.
- I'll provide a repeatable process for effective IT satisfaction measurement, monitoring, and improvement. It'll give you a straightforward and effective method to achieve IT satisfaction.
- You'll learn how to develop an actionable IT satisfaction improvement plan that identifies the causes of digital friction and outlines how to reduce it. Finally, you'll get the tools that tell you and your team exactly how much money, time, and other resources you need to improve satisfaction levels, employee engagement, and retention, leading to increased profits.
- Plus, you'll learn how to prioritize delivering satisfaction and discover that satisfaction can be awesome (it is!)

I wrote this book specifically for you, someone with the ambition and ability to revolutionize the digital employee experience for your team, group, function, business, or enterprise:

- A CEO, CTO, or other senior business leader who feels that IT could do more to give your company a competitive advantage.

- An IT leader who wants to take action on employee and IT satisfaction survey results to make IT changes that benefit employees and the business but doesn't know how.
- A business Marketing or Sales executive who senses their customers aren't happy and needs help figuring out why.
- An HR leader dealing with high turnover, difficulty hiring, low morale, and increasing recruitment costs.
- A Customer Success Manager stuck in the middle between business and end-customers and seeing the tension first-hand.

Leading with satisfaction to boost DEX is an excellent IT strategy.

Above all, if you want your business to thrive, you must ensure that digital employees are productive and, thus, happy. That means leading with satisfaction so you can match what they expect with your IT delivery.

> "Strategy becomes the particular array of activities aligned to deliver a particular mix of value to a chosen array of customers."
>
> — *Michael Porter*

Use digital employee satisfaction as your guide. Your "true north" should be your employees using digital workplace solutions without hassles.

When it comes to IT solutions, employees are the ones who know where the issues are. As an IT leader, it's essential to understand what they expect of IT and how they perceive IT — these two things aren't always the same. If IT isn't providing a more than adequate experience, dissatisfaction is the symptom, not the cause.

To boost the value IT brings to your company's business goals, you must understand why your solutions are vital to employees: the business outcomes and the individual needs of every team — Sales, CSM, IT, and other business or IT functions.

You need to lead with satisfaction as your compass to diagnose the root cause of dissatisfaction and where your IT service strategy, design, transition, and operations functions broke down.

Dissatisfaction leaves a trail of clues to its causes — if you know where to look.

IT can cause problems; we all know this. Whether it's slow systems, outdated software, or frequent crashes, it's frustrating when technology gets in the way of our work. As someone who's been there, I know that IT dissatisfaction can be a real business problem.

But I also found out that dissatisfaction contains the secret to our success. By paying attention to the signs of IT dissatisfaction, you can uncover the root causes of the problem and take steps to fix it.

Here are some tips on recognizing the clues and using them to improve your IT systems and boost your business performance. Let's dive into the world of IT dissatisfaction!

- **Your business employee productivity is falling.** Do digital employees in companies with 6+ communication tools, 10+

apps, and multiple SaaS services truly spend 5 hours per week in support? Yes, they do! And to make matters worse, it can take over 9 minutes to get back into a workflow after switching between workplace applications. On top of that, the average digital employee changes contexts up to 400 times a day! These work disruptions — and that's what they are — could be a problem for businesses that need their employees to be able to handle more work as they grow.

- **Your profitability and cash flow are shrinking.** Do your IT investments help you stay ahead of the competition? Keeping up with IT innovation and delivering satisfying employee experiences is critical to staying competitive and boosting your profits. Not investing in IT can lead to unhappy end-customers, low morale, difficulty recruiting and keeping top talent, lowering productivity, and costs you market share and profits.

- **You need help figuring out how to resolve dissatisfaction.** Are your business customers grumbling that things need fixing? Are survey response rates dropping? Are conversations with business unit heads getting a bit heated? If so, you may have a satisfaction issue caused by digital friction, and you should reexamine your approach.

- **Employee morale is low, and you have difficulty recruiting and retaining talent.** Digital friction is a top cause of low morale because employees can't get their job done, affecting their self-esteem and ability to succeed personally and professionally.

- **Your company needs to improve end-customer satisfaction and loyalty.** When employees are disengaged, it shows up as low external customer satisfaction in your marketplace.

When employees have trouble using your IT solutions or don't get the help they need, it affects your business and profits. So, please, get to know them! Ask them what you can do to help. Talk to them directly, and rely on something other than summaries from others.

Finding a disconnect between your understanding and theirs could signify a satisfaction issue that needs addressing immediately.

Leading with satisfaction is well worth your time and effort — and it takes little of it.

Completely Satisfied shows you how to give your internal customers and employees IT experiences that fulfill their expectations without relying on inflexible "best practices." I'll give you insights and explain how to satisfy your employees and customers quickly.

I'll show you how to turn your most disgruntled employees into ardent supporters. You'll learn how to adjust the IT value chain to deliver an experience that puts and keeps digital employees "in the zone" to give your company a competitive advantage.

Start where you are — right now!

All IT leaders measure employee satisfaction in some way, but many lack an understanding of what drives satisfaction or dissatisfaction.

By understanding your drivers of IT dissatisfaction, you can measure and monitor DEX more effectively, gain actionable insights, and learn where and how to make changes to your IT solutions and delivery to satisfy your employees and their internal and external partners.

As an IT leader, you have the power to take ownership of empowering your team and driving innovation that enhances digital employee experience.

By exploring new approaches and strategies — like those in this book — you can make a real difference in the success of your organization.

> "I always get to where I'm going by walking away from where I have been."
>
> —*Winnie the Pooh*

The place to start is improving IT satisfaction for IT solutions (aka, IT products and services) already in production. The "10 Steps" assume you've got one or more such opportunities, and the sequence of steps is remedial. Their order will differ if you're building a new service from scratch. For instance, you would start with Step 8 and create your service concept, a business and experience-centric blueprint!

So, let's start where you are by sorting out what satisfaction looks like and why delivering it can be tricky. Let's figure out precisely what you're trying to accomplish so we can make sure everyone's completely satisfied — you, your team and business partners, and of course, your employees.

1

WHAT SATISFACTION IS AND IS NOT

SATISFACTION AS PERCEPTION

Perception is critical to understanding our experiences, whether attending a concert or evaluating satisfaction with IT services.

Concerts are live performances, so you never know what'll happen. Imagine you've been waiting years to see your favorite performer and are finally about to see them live. Watching them tune up, you wonder if they'll play well. Will they be "on" tonight? You're excited and can't wait for them to start.

But once the music begins, it's obvious this isn't their best night. You keep hoping it'll get better, but they're off, and you're pretty disappointed.

When we have a terrible experience like this concert, we think about why it was so bad. Unsurprisingly, it was because the band didn't meet our expectations — they were unreliable, unresponsive, didn't keep their promises, weren't engaging or understanding, and sounded pretty awful! That's why we feel so dissatisfied.

The same rules apply to IT digital workplace solutions, products, and services. Investing in strategy, design, transition, and operation decisions can make or break the user experience.

> "Digital employees, not the Information Technology department, determine and define quality and value."

— Adapted from Heskett, Sasser, and Schlesinger's "The Service Profit Chain"

If someone's not satisfied with what you've delivered, it's time to step back and figure out whom it impacts and why it matters.

Remember that while tech is essential, people's issues of perception matter most when it comes to satisfaction — just like a live concert.

Changing your perception can dramatically change how you view satisfaction and IT.

A perception shift can help us to hone in on what's important to each person and why. When we start to invest in understanding digital employee expectations and perceptions, IT shifts from talking about faceless "users" to real people with names, unique stories, feelings, and business goals.

> "We are what we repeatedly do. Excellence then is not an act, but a habit."
>
> *— Aristotle*

When we change our perspective, we can quickly determine what our digital employees need, spot hidden solutions to problems, discover opportunities we may have missed, and make better choices.

Leading with Satisfaction can transform how you think about IT and deliver IT solutions.

Check out the example below from the MIT Sloan Management Review article "Finishing Off IT" (*sloanreview.mit.edu/article/finishing-off-it/*) — it's a great example of how IT leaders can benefit from perception switching!

***

Background: Liberty Mutual IT set out to run IT like a business by transforming, aligning with its business, and improving external customer engagement and loyalty.

Perception Switching: Stephen Wrenn, then AVP of IT Service Management at Liberty Mutual Insurance, said, "The IT department learned that its Sunday maintenance schedule interfered with external customers who wanted to check quotes and conduct other business online during the weekend. IT changed its schedule to accommodate their needs." He added, "These are value-added differentiators. IT has actually focused ... to help drive customer service and performance improvements."

Results: Liberty Mutual implemented a project reorganizing IT activity to accommodate customers' weekend needs. This resulted in increased customer retention and satisfaction and improved the efficiency, effectiveness, and economy of dependent non-IT organizations. Liberty Mutual's revenue increased by $477 million compared to the same period in the year earlier (before the change was made.)

Conclusion: Edmund F. Kelly, then Liberty Mutual Chairman, President, and CEO, said, "I am pleased with our financial results in the quarter. Revenue growth reflects higher retention of existing accounts and very satisfactory new business growth."

***

Those who do the work know best how to do it — and what they need to get it done.

It's no secret that IT service value chains are more complex than ever. Nor that we often measure how well our technology works by gauging employee satisfaction. But we need to remember that we're the ones providing these services, so it's essential to put ourselves in the shoes of our business employees using them.

We need to ensure we're providing a great experience by taking special care in designing and delivering our IT solutions, products, and services to ensure satisfaction. Yep, we're ditching IT "speeds and feeds" and jumping into the world of feelings and emotions — say hello to psychometrics!

Psychometrics is mood-altering psychology for that IT satisfaction.

Psychometrics is a branch of psychology that measures psychological attributes and can evaluate how thoughts and attitudes influence experiences. This includes assessing satisfaction levels, such as how satisfied someone is with IT (or a concert!)

In IT satisfaction, psychometrics involves using psychological measurement techniques to assess attitudes specifically related to information technology experiences.

It's also a significant shift for most of us. It's new, but as digital savviness grows, so do employee expectations for personalized work experiences. It's our job to measure these expectations and use them to improve the services and solutions we provide.

We must take a holistic view of our employees' mental models to manage expectations. We need to understand the nuances of their preferences, values, and motivations. Psychometrics can help us here.

Psychometrics is an approach that can help us determine how people interact with our digital workplace solutions and how they use them. We can use this data to design IT experiences tailored to each IT workgroup, leading to higher engagement and better business results.

By the way, you're likely already collecting data from your employees to create psychometric profiles — you probably call them IT satisfaction scores! No matter what you call it, you can start using your data to understand digital employee sentiment — how they feel IT is doing. All of this requires lots of listening. We must talk to our employees, ask them questions, and learn from them. We need to be open to feedback and recognize that our employees might have different perspectives than us. We must also be aware of and control our biases. After all, digital employees know best what they need to do their job, not us in IT!

Once we clearly understand how our employees view the digital workplace solutions we provide them, we can start to design services and solutions that meet their expectations.

Psychometrics is how we create custom-tuned experiences that drive better business results.

Disconfirmation is satisfaction's litmus test!

Disconfirmation is how we determine whether we're satisfied (or not.) Unfamiliar words describing a different way of working can be intimidating since they're new and unknown to us. Should we hang back or plunge in when we see words like psychometrics and disconfirmation? In this case, we need to look into them.

Why? Because disconfirmation reflects the science behind the satisfaction we feel from experiences. Our brains constantly make comparisons without realizing it, and disconfirmation is how we do it.

Even a world-class IT function can get it wrong without the proper perspective.

From an IT provider's point of view, we know what we're creating is valuable. We invest millions in the latest tech, cloud hosting, office applications, software dev tools, and support desks.

But that doesn't mean anything to salespeople who can't take orders or remote workers who can't log in because of IT problems. To them, it's just digital friction — yet another IT letdown.

It's a new experience for some of us, but we must understand how employees view our services to change our point of view. Things have changed drastically in recent years, and if we want to move forward, we need to work with our digital employees to meet their expectations. We must stop defining satisfaction by what we measure and start defining it by how our employees measure us.

We'll continue working as always if we don't develop that perspective. And we know that without a new approach, we're not doing our best to empower our employees, customers, and company.

"Stop defining satisfaction by what you measure and start defining it by how your employees measure you."

— *Completely Satisfied*

IT folks must now learn to measure themselves through the feelings of those they serve — and that's a leap of faith for some. But the winners in every industry, market, and location recognized that while evaluating IT solutions using traditional metrics is essential, more is needed.

We also know that to get an accurate picture of satisfaction, we need to measure IT from the outside — by gauging employee experience against expectations. As the clock ticks and economic realities become more pressing, those who refuse to accept the importance of leading with satisfaction are getting passed over by those that do.

Don't fall into that trap. Recognize the value of measuring satisfaction, perception, and experience.

Perception Pitfalls

IT leaders can get stuck in the mindset that there's only one way to get a digital business solution up and running, and that's how IT has always worked. These leaders believe that working with digital employees isn't worth the effort, or only if we're not on a tight timeline and then only by engaging "Superusers" — who don't represent the average user by definition! These leaders also tend to focus on the technical side of the solution too.

For example, when kicking off a new digital workplace initiative or CRM solution, could insights from average users on the front lines benefit your IT projects even more? Would your CRM tool be better if you got feedback from the customer contact people who use it daily, and even better if you understood how external customers of those employees interact with those employees and their results expectations? I bet you could.

But if we don't prioritize and lead with satisfaction, we tend to double down on the wrong things. We've gotten stuck in our way of thinking without even noticing because it's what's worked for us in the past. It's what we know. That's why it can be tough to shift gears once we fall into that rut. We tend to stick to what we know without even thinking about it.

We need to break these habits and learn to broaden our perspective, looking at both the operational and the emotional sides of IT solution production and consumption. IT perception pitfalls leading to poor IT satisfaction usually come in two broad forms but stem from the same source.

Perception Pitfall 1: You start with technology and don't realize success requires something else.

The first leadership pitfall is not starting with the customer and working backward toward the technology.

Instead, most IT failures start because of leading with technology — from choosing a solution and working outward from IT toward the employee and customer, trying to determine how to make your chosen solution fit them. Force-fitting technology is a recipe for disaster.

Let's examine the ways this approach goes wrong.

Imagine you're an IT leader pressed with the mandate of "digital transformation." It's your mission to digitize the workplace, and you decide it will be a state-of-the-art solution — you know how to roll out hardware and software; it's what you do!

Without realizing it, you just made a series of critical decisions with long-term consequences when you made this a technology project:

1. **Your business, employees, and customers.** Your approach will build a technology-centric solution, and your metrics reflect IT operational status. Employees will find it increasingly stressful and challenging to deliver their business products and services to external customers. You should expect lower employee productivity, engagement, and IT satisfaction due to increased digital friction and lack of insight into employee quality of experience.

2. **Alternatives and competitive solutions.** Your employees and customers have choices, and you compete with other businesses regarding employee retention and customer loyalty. You can expect to see problems recruiting and higher turnover of your staff and digital employees. Lost customers and market position usually follow — who likes paying to engage with disgruntled employees using a clunky IT solution?

3. **Service concept.** You've just set expectations and a roadmap for your solution, and it won't be easy to change functionality or support later. When IT satisfaction starts falling, you'll likely have to get a new understanding of employee and customer needs and expectations. You'll need to patch things up with new systems and processes to meet those lacking capabilities arising from disconnects between your plan, build, transition, and run teams.

As you start rolling out your new IT solution, you end up with something you didn't plan on. Employee satisfaction and productivity starts falling, along with customer retention, loyalty, and profits.

While adding some new software and a couple of workflows doesn't sound like that much change, you've created a more complex workplace for employees and increased digital friction to the point that employees quit and customers are not getting the service and interactions they demand. Your solution hasn't changed much, but everything about its experience has.

Why? Because you didn't take into account employee perceptions around the solution. You didn't change your perspective and "lead with satisfaction."

Your perceptions about your IT solution can change everything (and they did for the worse in the preceding example.)

Now, imagine if you had changed your point of view and led with satisfaction instead:

1. **Your business, employees, and customers.** You co-create an experience-centric solution. Employees helped you refine and optimize critical areas that make delivering your business products and services easier and faster to external customers. With user guidance, you removed several options and made others defaults, reducing digital friction. Higher employee productivity leads to improved customer loyalty.
2. **Alternatives and competitive solutions.** Your company now has a competitive edge, and retention is higher as employees are more engaged. Your more user-centric solution creates a more "can-do" and customer-friendly atmosphere.
3. **Service concept.** You worked with digital employees to understand how they work with customers to develop your

service concept, prioritizing capabilities and adding new ways of working and tools. Your service concept outlines the business goals (and metrics) of all involved. IT Strategy, design, transition, and run functions work together without hiccups. Your metrics reflect employee satisfaction and business goals.

Before choosing a solution, you waged a battle for the experience of your new digital workplace. Your new solution drives retention of your employees, customer loyalty, and business profitability. Feedback from sales and marketing is that external customers are talking about how easy and pleasant it is to do business with your company because you took the time to build the solution needed. I think you know how they feel now!

"Producer and consumer ... share data, information, knowledge, and wisdom ... and fuse into a prosumer."

— *Toffler*

So, as an IT leader, you might not see too much difference between your old workplace solution and the new — it's almost the same, right? However, deliberately choosing a producer-consumer (prosumer) point of view results in two very different service concepts.

IT, meet prosumer; prosumer, meet IT.

Prosumerism in IT encourages collaboration between users and IT. They work together to tailor IT products, services, and solutions.

Users get more control over their workplace, and IT can align their company solutions with company business goals. Prosumerism requires a user-centered approach to get digital employee input and feedback. You then use their insights to create customized solutions that improve productivity and satisfaction. It leads to better innovation, efficiency, and user satisfaction.

By choosing prosumerism, you've directly impacted productivity, employee and customer retention, and your business's profits — only this time for the better!

The result is solutions that meet user needs and help the organization be successful.

Your perspective is a real game-changer, so play your cards right.

As IT leaders, we all need to understand that our unconscious biases and perspectives drive our choices and have a cascading business impact — positive or negative.

The success of past IT solutions can trap you. But know that what worked well in the past isn't necessarily what the present requires, especially not for digital transformation. Today IT success takes a very different approach to the workplace.

When you decide what you want to deliver — a state-of-the-art digital workplace solution, for example — you can't forge on as you did in the past. You have to stop and think about the service concept. That means starting with external customers, working backward through digital employees, understanding the results they need to succeed, what value means, and designing for experience. After that, you'll understand the desired outcomes from the eyes of employees and end-customers, and then you can turn your attention back to technology.

We often get this reversed because we lose the end-customer and employee perspective and, in our technology-driven enthusiasm, rush to complete a project because it's what we've learned to do.

Perception Pitfall 2: You designed your IT solution based on your understanding of expectations, but they've changed.

The second pitfall is using outdated understandings of business, customers, results, and employees in your design and strategy development.

You get trapped by your perceptions of how things used to work. Your IT solutions and how you measure them exist within a business context — obvious enough. The trouble is that business contexts and how your external (end) customers perceive them constantly change.

As our external customers evolve their preferences, our companies adapt to those market changes. Our employees and the solutions we build and deliver to them must adapt. For that, we must adjust. Have yours? Have you?

> "The only thing worse than being blind is having sight but no vision."
>
> — *Helen Keller*

For example, consider your technology monitoring solutions. They form the core of IT metrics and how most of us predict employee satisfaction today. They're insufficient now. They're essential, but IT *Quality of Service* (QoS) approaches measure operational metrics. They don't provide insights into humanistic digital employee experience perceptions (QoE.) You'll do best with both today.

And sometimes, a great solution suddenly finds itself out of favor, not because it's changed but because its context in the workplace has shifted. Consider messaging morphing into virtual meetings. Adding more technology that does the same thing doesn't make much sense. Yet we continue to pile on evermore messaging solutions — consider the proliferation of Microsoft Teams, Cisco WebEx, Zoom, Slack, Amazon Chime, and others.

This explosion of "choices" has increased context shifting and workplace configuration time. Most employees now spend 10-15% of meeting time trying to get video and audio settings to function. Add the number of attendees' two-factor (2FA) and multi-factor (MFA) authentications. Multiply that by the number of meetings — it adds up quickly, and that's just for meetings. Think about all the logins and settings across your entire digital workplace solution and multiply that by all the IT solutions you provide.

Research shows that today employees lose about five (5!) weeks per year task switching, context switching, and fighting digital friction. In the preceding virtual meeting solutions example, we had an excellent messaging solution and forgot to account for the added complexity. What started as giving employees choice turned into a tower of babble.

Now, your once-popular menu of digital workplace meeting solutions seems out of sync with what makes your digital employees productive — and it negatively affects their ability to work with end-customers because of all the context switching. Your technical metrics tell you all those systems are well. But what would your employees tell you instead?

Our employees work in a context that's often quite different from ours. As we look at our favorite reports, it's easy to miss a workplace change that negatively impacts our customer-facing employees, such as sales, or those working internally, like HR, for example.

Finding yourself trapped is today's central IT problem: The business proposition changed, but the IT proposition and viewpoints remained the same. You've been trapped by your original thinking even though the workplace has moved on.

How to Lead with Satisfaction Like Your Job Depends on It — Because it Does

The failure pattern shared by these pitfalls and examples is not deliberately leading with satisfaction, not considering employees and the end-customers they work with, and not designing the experience you need to deliver.

The root cause is not consciously shifting our perspectives to include our producer-consumer relationships' technical and emotional sides. We need to think "prosumer," but we don't.

Why is this so common? Why do we often stick with our "default" perspective, even when our technology and business environments change?

Over my career, I've found a standard answer: no one taught us that every experience has a producer and consumer. Of course, we know that experiences don't just happen, but we haven't recognized that and shifted our point of view on it to make it our "new normal."

Satisfaction with digital experiences can only occur when we're bi-directionally aligned. Our consumers can only signal to us that something makes them unhappy, less productive, or less engaged. As producers, we have to respond to those signals, but we haven't, and we don't know how because we're not soliciting them in actionable ways.

We know this because if we look back at any enterprise, we see that collections of people work towards providing something of value for an audience. We understand how business works. Yet, we fall into our "default" perception and struggle with outdated approaches because it's what we know best. We say we prioritize business user satisfaction and align IT with business goals, but our business customers and users say we're not.

Let's look at the difference between "default" technology-centric IT and deliberate customer-centric (prosumer) solution design and leading with satisfaction.

Imagine this time you start by asking about employees and their end-customers — you measure the digital friction employees face and its impact on those end-customers in your marketplace. Then you think about employee experience and *Business Value at Risk* (BVaR).

As a result, picking up the preceding messaging example again, instead of adding new messaging tools and apps, you reduce them to the ones the workgroup employees use most — not the ones IT uses or one or two loud Superuser voices champion.

Then, by talking with these employees, you learn they need quick answers to crucial customer questions and so add new knowledge to your support systems. What a difference. The same technology, but now with fitness for use and purpose optimized to reduce employee stress.

You're leading with satisfaction!

We fail when we don't "lead with satisfaction," and we often take the way we know best in a pinch.

The preceding was a simple example, but we'll keep doing things the same way without a perception shift. We must drop the idea that IT knows what's best and that as long as we measure what we do today, we're doing what's best for employees, customers, and business partners. We must unlearn this incorrect behavior if we're to be successful.

We must force ourselves by deliberately stepping outside our technology comfort zone and into the world of emotions. That small step requires commitment, time, and, most importantly, a systematic approach to satisfying DEX expectations.

While collaboration solutions gave a simple example of digital friction, we do the same with our other more complex IT solutions. We make decisions without an inclusive perception of experience or satisfaction and paint ourselves into a corner without even knowing it — then we wonder what's wrong with those pesky users! Integrating operational and humanistic perceptions can improve outcomes for all involved, but we've not yet learned how to do that.

It works two ways. In the Liberty Mutual example, they were under-delivering — causing lost sales and churn. It's also possible to over-deliver with similarly poor business results. An excellent example of this failure is my work with a Global IT service provider, as seen in this *Satisfaction Story*.

***

Satisfaction Story: *IT Service Provider Over-delivery Cannibalizing Sales*

Background: A networking professional services company accessed customer-premise equipment to diagnose and fix problems remotely. They sold services primarily by time to resolve. The mantra was "people before process" and "the customer is always right" — their goal was customer satisfaction, so they spent significant time staring at operational metrics. Their primary metric was time to close an incident. That led to team competitiveness. They were a service-focused organization where everyone was having fun (except sales.) The problem was that sales of their more expensive services were falling while sales of the lowest level service were increasing.

Results: We found the sales problem when we shifted perspectives and engaged sales employees. IT support engineers were proud to solve problems quickly and raced to see who could solve the most problems without regard for customer response time agreements. They had made the low-tier service as effective as the highest. Simply put, they didn't understand their company's business model, and their IT service concept was putting their business out of business.

Conclusion: Their shift in perspective changed how IT worked, drove sales, and got them acquired at a nice multiple. Letting solved tickets lay open was tough, but they all understood they were losing sales by over-delivering. Nothing feels so alien as delivering on time, something you could provide sooner. Yet by consciously changing perspective and optimizing work processes, they could find problems fast and sequence the solution to fall within bands defined by their offerings. *They designed the experience they needed to deliver.*

***

Employee or customer experience differs from satisfaction, and digital employee experience efforts must be for the right reasons.

Sales satisfaction in the prior Satisfaction Story was low, while end-customers were quite pleased with the service they received. But it was putting my client out of business, and honestly, customers knew that restoration times were much faster than promised. So did sales, and that's the point.

If management had listened to sales staff and coordinated with internal business partners, they could have solved the problem before it negatively affected the business.

> "To change ourselves effectively, we first had to change our perceptions."
>
> — *Stephen Covey*

The previous examples show that profitable experiences only happen when all parties to the service concept are satisfied. In both instances, they had to consider employees and customers to maintain satisfaction, engineer the desired experience, and improve business agility and outcomes.

What matters to an employee is being able to do their job when and where they need to do it. What matters to end-customers (and every employee!) is getting value from the services and products you and your IT workers deliver. Anything that gets in the way lowers your consumers perceived quality of experience. For employees, that's a loss of productivity and engagement, and looking for a new employer. For external customers, that's reconsidering their loyalty and your company's value proposition.

So finally, we see our conundrum. Our IT metrics look great, but employees and external customers are dissatisfied. From my service provider client example, you saw how operational metrics can even drive the wrong behavior. Over-delivering is just as bad as under-delivering.

There's no room today for unearned IT or business errors. How you manage your IT solutions underpins your business strategy and can mean the difference between success and failure, personally and professionally.

But there's a zone within which any IT solution must operate. Its name is the *Zone of Tolerance* or ZoT for short — we'll learn more about the ZoT in Step 6.

Stop Trying to Delight IT Users (Because You Can't)

Lots of IT organizations face these same complex problems. It's tough not to give in to the desire to try to delight employees. But this can be expensive and as bad for the organization as not doing enough!

> "How to succeed: try hard enough. How to fail: try too hard."
>
> — *Malcolm Forbes*

The costs associated with delighting IT users often outweigh the potential benefits, and user productivity is unlikely to improve significantly.

Plus, in today's enterprise environment, IT users are often restricted in their ability to customize their IT experience due to organizational standards and policies. They most likely won't ever be delighted.

But they can be completely satisfied. And when they are, IT and our solutions become a utility, like lights, HVAC, and the Internet. Our solutions must be ready and taken for granted when employees need them and otherwise forgotten about unless they're not working.

Keeping IT delivery in the zone where employees are most productive makes the most sense. This way, digital employees can meet their needs without IT wasting money on unnecessary extras, money better spent improving DEX!

Making IT work without breaking the bank.

We must remember the importance of balance and cost-effectiveness for enterprise IT. A forward-thinking approach to technology investments can result in long-term cost savings and improved operational efficiency.

Balancing cost-effectiveness and meeting IT users' critical technology needs is essential. You must provide a stable, reliable, and up-to-date technology infrastructure that enables employees to perform their tasks efficiently and effectively.

You can optimize productivity and promote a positive work culture by prioritizing digital employee experience, understanding the zone of tolerance for meeting core requirements, and ensuring consistent delivery within that zone.

The bottom line is that it's not worth it for most IT leaders to attempt to delight IT users, nor is it helpful to be too frugal. It makes more sense to keep IT users where they can effectively use the technology to meet their needs without additional costs.

This approach helps the organization save money and ensures that IT users can use technology to the best of their ability.

Okay! I'm Sold on Leading with Satisfaction. How Do I Do It?

Considering how necessary managing employee experience and satisfaction is and how long the concept has been around, you would think there's an accepted methodology. Well, you're correct. There is!

There are frameworks describing user experience, satisfaction, QoS (the producer view), and QoE (the consumer view), and they've been evolving for 30+ years. The problem is that it's something you have to do. You have to "own" it and make it happen. You have to lead with satisfaction to achieve satisfaction. You can't buy, install, and forget DEX. It's not a tool or something you outsource.

Leading with satisfaction requires changing how you manage delivery and your IT function. And it may go against everything you've learned working in IT. Still, at first, adding humanistic measures isn't a big deal because you'll continue using your old QoS metrics, and the new QoE metrics you start collecting are numbers too. But then everything starts to change, and you start thinking differently.

Why? Because you'll have changed your perspective from inside looking outward — to outside looking inward.

Change your view, change your game.

The shift in your vantage point changes how you see your IT solutions and manage their delivery.

1. **Digital employees become individuals:** You will build emotional connections with real people who depend upon your decision-making; they'll no longer be annoying anonymous "users" but co-workers with names, stories, and unique needs. The truth is that digital employees didn't build the digital workplace they must use — you did. So, if satisfaction is low, it means your QoE is low. Take ownership.

2. **You'll see why external customers value your company:** You'll realize you don't fully understand what digital employees need or do to be successful. To ensure high-quality delivery, IT leaders must understand the expectations of digital employees and their external customers. Failing to meet those expectations could lead to being replaced by external service providers who understand even less well what digital workers need.

3. **Set the proper IT solution quality standards:** When you realize your solution's quality strategy isn't meeting the expectations of digital workers, you'll panic (a little) and wonder why. You must understand what digital employees and their customers expect from IT and convert that knowledge into meaningful design standards for your team to measure and manage.

4. **Confirm that IT performance meets standards:** Once you've got a sound design, you'll need to verify that what you plan is what you deliver — and usually, even if unintended, that's not what happens. Disconnects between planning,

building, delivering, and communicating about your IT solutions are generally the most common issues. You can find that while you've set standards, IT isn't meeting them. Fortunately, this is easy to identify, rectify, and manage — and all it takes is a bit of leadership intensity. Lean into it.

5. **Track IT delivery to ensure it matches promises:** By this point, your solution's experience should be solid. The next issue is that IT communications (official or otherwise) often reset digital worker expectations higher (making it tougher to meet them.) It's common for IT to overpromise by saying one thing and delivering another. When what you provide doesn't match these new expectations, you're right back at the starting point with a dissatisfied digital employee.

Solve satisfaction — IT style!

Here's the bottom line. Many IT managers work under strained relations with their businesses. Designing experiences that satisfy can be a big and somewhat complex task. But don't worry; it becomes much easier when we take it in logical chunks and work through them using simple examples.

Let's break down the complexity of engineering satisfaction.

THE 5+2 COMPONENTS OF EXPERIENCE SATISFACTION

Measuring IT satisfaction is an established concept. Yet most IT satisfaction surveys don't produce actionable results because they can't identify which factors contribute to dissatisfaction — they're not diagnostic.

We struggle to measure IT satisfaction because we've never learned how to do it correctly or have ineffective, sometimes counterproductive tools.

Enter the IT satisfaction smooth talker, the survey. Somewhere along the way, satisfaction surveys became synonymous with measuring digital employee experience, but they're not. We've confused how to measure IT satisfaction (a moment in time) with how to analyze IT quality of experience (satisfaction over time.)

Ask any IT leader, and most will say they measure satisfaction. Yet most of us in IT need more exposure and expertise in leading with satisfaction. We wing or delegate it, and as you saw from my previous examples, not knowing what we're doing can be dangerous and counterproductive.

Why you should never create a satisfaction survey.

While PZB did a great job introducing QoE and placing satisfaction in its proper context, it was more of a research tool for high-end services marketing than a corporate IT solution. That's why traditional satisfaction surveys like NPS, CES, and CSAT came to fill the gap between QoS and QoE.

Satisfaction (and experience) surveys are delicate instruments, subject to misinterpretation. Your goal is noble — to measure digital employees' thoughts about IT, its products, or services. You're seeking an assessment of how they feel about specific outcomes your solution is supposed to provide so you can take action.

But here's an example of one of the most common surveys IT uses today (and an excellent example of what not to do):

"How would you rate your satisfaction level with us?"

What's wrong with that traditional homemade IT CSAT question, you ask? Let me turn this around: what action can you take with the survey results? What do you compare it to? What does good look like? What do the results tell you?

I know you've felt this frustration before!

The primary problem is that IT satisfaction is relative, subjective — and emotional! Nevertheless, you need to know the upper and lower boundaries of expectations based on desired outcomes for each workgroup. Then, your IT satisfaction score will look more like the image in Figure I-1, which is probably quite different from what you're familiar with.

FIGURE I-1. IT Satisfaction "Barometer" Shows Satisfaction Relative to Expectations

When I show Figure I-1 to most people, it causes them to stop and think. They notice that satisfaction isn't delight or dissatisfaction. It's more like "productive" with an absence of dissatisfaction. But it's not how they view IT satisfaction today or how their shiny new tools report it.

Surprised? A bit worried about your own ITCSAT surveys? Here are ten more reasons why asking someone if they're satisfied can be a bit pointless:

- Hesitancy in providing honest feedback
- Limited understanding of the question or its context
- Potential misinterpretation of the question leading to skewed results
- Influence of current mood, situation, or last interaction on the response
- Lack of time or inclination to respond
- Difficulty in quantifying satisfaction without additional

context or information

- Bias in responses when asked the same question multiple times
- Unreliable data due to a small sample size
- Skewed answers because of asking similar questions in different ways
- Pressure or bias to provide a positive response

Here's a real-world example of the dangers of satisfaction surveys.

Many well-meaning IT managers and highly skilled IT analysts confuse some basic concepts, leading to the ever-widening "business-IT gap."

Like all fields, IT satisfaction is more profound than you'd think it could be. Because of its nuances, measuring IT satisfaction is one area of IT in which most have no professional experience.

You probably know how it feels if you work in IT. You use IT satisfaction surveys to "measure quality." You've likely got popups in all your apps asking how happy employees are. You randomly pester users to complete a survey after every call to the Service Desk, and you do a mass email a few times a year.

Few users complete your surveys, but those that do generally indicate satisfaction with the transaction (usually not great, but not too far down in the dumps either.)

But your users, customers, and business partners still complain about poor IT quality of experience. What gives?

Funny as it sounds, one may be satisfied with a transaction (a moment in time) and still feel that QoE (satisfaction over time) is low.

The following Satisfaction Story is a simple example from my own experience.

***

Satisfaction Story: *Dan the Cable Guy*

Background: My Internet failed several times a month mysteriously. It would slowly degrade, with my download speeds falling. I paid for top-tier boosted high-speed service. You could say my expectations for service were high since, according to what my provider had told me via its marketing and what they charged me for it, I should have been delighted with the quality of service I received, but I wasn't.

Results: I was occasionally satisfied with the support I got, even though when I called the Service Desk, they made me wade through a litany of troubleshooting steps, asked dozens of questions, and then always reset my cable modem. (I knew they were following ITIL's good practices, and I told myself that, in the long run, it was good for me.) Still, I was dissatisfied with the Service Desk since they never resolved the issue and wasted my time. But they always sent Technician Dan (not his real name.) Dan was good at what he did and respected my home by wearing booties that kept my carpet clean. Dan solved my problems, so I was satisfied when Dan came and fixed things.

Conclusion: Let me be clear. If my provider asked me about the quality of my Internet service (which they never did), I would've said without hesitation that it was poor and I was not getting my money's worth. This service interrupted my work and made me take on a troubleshooting job for them — wasting more of my time. Based on what they told me I was supposed to get for what I paid, I felt like I was getting ripped off. I would have answered "no" if they asked me if I would recommend them to a friend (but they didn't). I did tell people to stay away from them, though, because their service quality was low, my experience was awful, and I was dissatisfied with them and their Internet service. Period. Now, if they asked me if I was satisfied with the service provided by Dan (which they always did!) I would, of course, say yes. Dan made an appointment, confirmed it, and showed up on time. Dan was efficient and pleasant, getting it done quickly without making a mess.

Discussion: Notice how I can be satisfied with one element of an IT solution (Dan's responsiveness, reliability, and empathy) yet still feel my provider, their Internet Service, and their Service Desk are poor? Can you see how there are better ways to measure QoE than seeking customer satisfaction after a call to the Service Desk? Did you spot the flaw in my service provider's logic? Since Dan has been here several times, if you trended my satisfaction (with Dan), you might think that service quality is high. And this is the mistake and trap of thinking that satisfaction with a transaction (e.g., Dan coming to "fix" my Internet connection) is equivalent to quality (QoE). It isn't, and it will never be so.

***

Now you know why you should never create a customer survey without having someone with a psychometric background evaluate your approach, environment (servicescape), and questions. If you don't, you could ask the wrong questions at the wrong time and get inaccurate or unhelpful information. Worse, you can get a false perception of your IT function and your digital employees!

> "Do what is easy, and your life will be hard. Do what is hard, and your life will become easy."
>
> — *Les Brown*

Instead, stick with approaches already proven. You can't "roll your own" and change words to "improve" a survey because it will probably cause more problems than it solves. Remember, commercial tools like CES, NPS, and SERVQUAL took years of refining to develop the approaches, questions, and even the order of asking them.

Have you got a problem with satisfaction surveys? Yeah, me too. We all do.

There's one more problem with simple surveys that ask if or how satisfied you are. Your results using such surveys could be as much as 35% off! Here's why. Anyone who spends time with NPS or CES runs into people who say they are satisfied (aka "loyal") but who switch brands or employment anyway. We also see some people who consistently express their "dissatisfaction." These folks account for roughly 25%-35% of people and, thus, 25%-35% of your satisfaction or loyalty values.

> "To the degree you give others what they need, they will give you what you need."
>
> — *Og Mandino*

Satisfaction is an emotional and subjective concept as it is — and that's why it's so problematic. But when you add in that a significant portion of survey respondents provide inaccurate responses about their IT satisfaction, it can have several implications for your data and what you decide to do based on the results:

- Our view of satisfaction and dissatisfaction is skewed.
- It's hard to get honest opinions and emotions.
- Spotting trends and patterns in the data is complex.

What does all this psychometric psycho-babble mean? It means mistakes, critical errors you must avoid. This is why you must be aware of the flaws of "satisfaction" surveys, shouldn't create your surveys, and must do all you can to reduce bias or, as the famous saying goes, "Trust but verify!"

Using the best tool for the job.

You might think that I don't like satisfaction or quality of experience surveys, but I do! When we know all the nuances and potential problem areas, they're fantastic tools, easy enough to use, and indispensable when used correctly.

The problems inherent in the common satisfaction measurement approaches also give us clues on how to do it right and turn results into something actionable. After all, isn't that the point? Why measure if we're not going to take action on what we find out, assuming that we want to find out something!

> "If all you have is a hammer, everything looks like a nail."
>
> — *Abraham Maslow*

There are good reasons to use any satisfaction survey — as long as you understand what you measure and do something meaningful with the results.

Most of the IT satisfaction tools you use today are okay to continue to use — but you probably should change how you use them. For example, NPS and CES are usually good at detecting dissatisfaction. Just don't use them to try to fix satisfaction; for that, you need something diagnostic, like SERVQUAL.

Be nimble, be quick, enabling business agility with each strategic pick.

Business agility refers to an organization's ability to swiftly recognize and respond to changes in the market, customer demands, technology, and other external factors. It emphasizes the capacity to effectively adjust strategies, processes, and resources to seize opportunities and navigate challenges in a fluid business environment.

When a business has agility, it's flexible, innovative, and resilient, allowing them to stay competitive and achieve sustainable growth. It involves fostering a culture of adaptability, empowering employees, leveraging data-driven insights, embracing new technologies, and implementing agile methodologies to drive continuous improvement and deliver value to customers.

> "Business agility is your mission, leading with IT satisfaction is your philosophy, and everything else you do as an IT leader is tactics."
>
> —*Completely Satisfied*

We can break down measuring satisfaction into five core components (plus two optional components) that define the actual quality of experience we deliver. We can then see precisely what we do well and not so well and what to change to deliver IT solutions (products and services) that improve DEX and drive business agility.

These are the Five (Plus Two) components of IT satisfaction and effective digital employee experience management:

1. **Perceptions.** The opinions employees form when using your IT solutions.

2. **Expectations.** What employees believe they'll experience using your IT solutions.
3. **The Zone of Tolerance.** The range of experience employees say they need to be productive.
4. **Disconfirmation.** How employees rate your IT solutions.
5. **Service Concept.** Linking your IT strategy to business value.
6. **(Bonus #1) Gaps Model.** Tools to diagnose digital employee experience failures and development treatments to remove root causes.
7. **(Bonus #2) Justification.** How to gain business support and funding for your IT satisfaction improvements.

1. Perceptions Shape Our Reality, and Our IT Solutions

I'm sure you already know how your employees feel when using your IT solutions. But do you take action on those feelings? How we interpret the usefulness of IT solutions like digital workplaces plays an essential role in determining digital employee experience.

"Knowledge is perception."

—*Theaetetus*

Whether positive or negative, our perceptions shape how we feel. If our perceptions are positive, we're likely to be more satisfied and have had a better experience; however, if our perceptions are negative, we may become dissatisfied, leading to a worse overall experience. For example, imagine your productivity suite's word processor kept changing your default font without you making any changes. You might be satisfied with its ability to print, but you hate that it keeps changing your fonts. Your perceptions don't fit your expectations.

If expectations fuel business value, perception is the engine of satisfaction, and that satisfaction over time represents your digital employee experience.

We unconsciously use five factors to decide if an experience satisfies our expectations. (That's a meaningful way to say it too.) They are, in their most common order of importance: Reliability, Responsiveness, Assurance, Empathy, and Tangibles. We use the clever acronym "RATER" to make them easy to remember.

RATER makes SERVQUAL diagnostic. Diagnostic means it tells you the source(s) and cause(s), hence the solutions of low satisfaction, essential to improving your delivery.

Here's an example. Let's say you're eager to take proactive steps when troubleshooting satisfaction issues. To do so effectively, you must capture accurate user perceptions and expectations. Using the RATER framework, you can analyze these factors and ensure they align with user expectations. RATER analysis helps you identify the areas of IT delivery that are falling short (e.g., one or more RATER factors), determine the extent of the shortcomings, and provide insights on what changes are needed.

For example, if Reliability is a -3, signaling high digital friction. You must bring it up to a 0 or possibly a +1 (see Figure I-1.) Taking direct action based on RATER analysis paves the way for improved satisfaction levels by reducing digital employee effort. You may need to change your maintenance window!

Experience is perception over time.

We leave every service encounter with a single satisfaction judgment. We unconsciously add up all those judgments to form the idea of quality, aka QoE, and that's what perception is.

And, like your GPA in school — QoE and DEX are easy to lower and harder to raise.

In Step 4, we'll discover how your IT solutions make employees feel and what it takes to satisfy them.

2. Expectations Define What Our IT Solutions Must Deliver and How

We all decide in advance what we want our experience to be — remember the concert example? Do you know what experiences digital employees need you to deliver and believe you'll provide? If not, you need to because digital employee expectations are our secret sauce in IT. It's how we can provide IT satisfaction that others cannot with solutions that drive growth, revenue, and retention. Unlike perceptions, expectations are easy to raise and harder to lower!

Expectations are what digital employees believe IT should deliver.

Digital employee experience, productivity, and profitability start by understanding consumers' expectations for your IT products and services. Expectations can be positive (e.g., the efficiency of service, quality of product, etc.) or negative (e.g., missing functionality, lack of customer service, and so on). They're the fuel that drives IT solutions and delivers business value and agility.

> "There were two ways to be happy: improve your reality, or lower your expectations."
>
> — *Jodi Picoult*

Expectations are vital to know for your services and digital workplace solutions. One size only fits some, and you can't assume what you want is what everyone else wants. For example, an IT engineer might cause their system to log out after a short period because they have privileged access. The engineer makes that the default for everyone. However, salespeople have long conversations with clients, and the timeout logs them out of the CRM system during their calls with clients, causing stress and digital friction.

Be careful about making assumptions. You can unwittingly damage IT satisfaction and productivity, but you can also quickly set expectations too high. Whatever you promise is what employees expect. And they don't forget either. Promises include what gets put in writing and whatever you and your team say or share.

The following Satisfaction Story shows how critical understanding, meeting, and managing expectations are to your success.

***

Satisfaction Story: *Managing Expectations Down for Profits*

Background: I worked with a leading provider of IT services with a diverse range of clients experiencing issues with customer satisfaction. Customers felt their service fell short of expectations, leading to dissatisfaction. Their expectations were too high because of over-enthusiastic marketing and sales communications.

Results: Lost clients and falling profits caused the team to discover and manage customer expectations to improve service quality. We used SERVQUAL and gained insights into customer expectations by reviewing marketing literature and customer feedback analysis. We identified personal needs, past experiences, word-of-mouth, marketing communications, and industry norms influencing customer expectations. Our goal became setting and meeting consistent delivery by managing customer expectations. But first, we had to reset expectations at the proper — sustainable — level.

Conclusion: They set realistic service standards based on customer expectations and developed clear benchmarks and metrics for service delivery. They ensured there was a single source of messaging for their services. Next, they improved service delivery by training staff, streamlining processes, and enhancing communication channels. Existing customers were at first unhappy, while new customers were quite satisfied. Over time customer satisfaction leveled out, as evidenced by higher customer feedback ratings, increased repeat business, and positive word-of-mouth referrals.

***

Expectation management is one area where I find IT leaders and teams dropping the ball, or worse, not knowing they have the ball! The preceding Satisfaction Story shows how important expectation management is to IT success. If you're not actively managing expectations, you've lost control and may have unhappy clients or be overspending.

We all have expectations. Our beliefs about what is possible and what we expect frame our experiences. We'll unpack how our minds work for (and against!) us in Step 5.

3. The Zone of Tolerance Sets the Boundaries of Cost, Performance, and IT Satisfaction

What level of IT performance do employees believe they need to be productive? You have established the upper and lower bounds of IT performance, correct? No? Welcome to the Zone of Tolerance or ZoT, as shown in Figure I-2.

FIGURE I-2. An Example of One Possible Zone of Tolerance

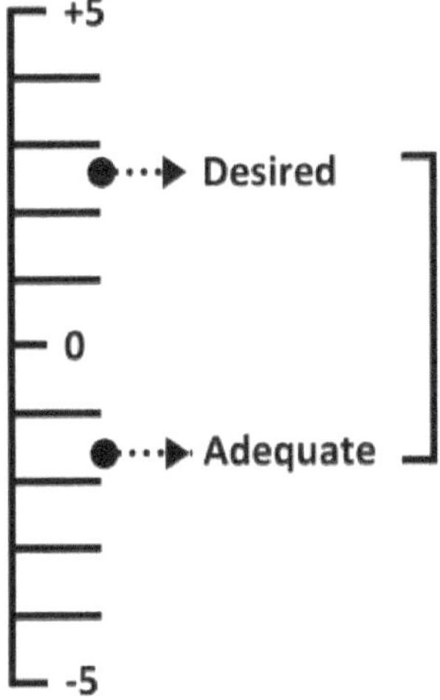

Figure I-2 shows the ZoT as a productivity window for your employees, business, and external customers. It's a scale representing desired performance at the top and what's adequate at the bottom. For example, imagine you're an Inside Sales Executive using the IT-provided Client Management System (CMS). As an AE, you look up records all day long. For the CMS to satisfy you and your client's needs, you probably can't wait more than 15-20 seconds for a record to load — your *Adequate* wait time. That's not ideal, though, because any longer than that starts to slow down your ability to meet your call quota and frustrates clients.

You've had excellent experiences with records appearing nearly instantly, however. So you know how fast the CMS can be, and your *Desired* wait time is less than a few seconds. But the system slows down during the day, and you know the best you will get is 5-6 seconds. The closer your perceived experience is to your expectations, the higher you would score the CMS on an IT satisfaction survey.

In this example, the difference between desired and adequate is the Zone of Tolerance for looking up a client record using the CMS.

> "There have been a few moments when I have known complete satisfaction, but only a few. I have rarely been free from the disturbing realization that my playing might have been better."
>
> — *Jan Ignace Paderewski*

You set the ZoT's scope as required. There are ZoTs for IT, groups (like service desk or application development), and solutions (as well as their services, products, and features).

Keep satisfaction in the "Zone" to satisfy users.

The positioning of your delivery in the zone sets off critical assumptions and actions. Figure I-2 shows how the Zone of Tolerance can mark out a range for delivery. It's a simple idea — discover the range from Adequate to Desired for actionable targets for performance management and then keep user perception "in the zone" between them to balance cost and value.

PZB argued that any service provider could outperform their competitors if they measure desired experience and then adjust delivery to meet those expectations.

So far, nearly 40 years later, SERVQUAL continues to be the global de-facto marketing approach. It's the gold standard, and it works for IT just as well as marketing.

The Zone of Tolerance concept defines the acceptable difference between expectations (Desired and Adequate) and real experience (Expected and Perceived.) Experiences falling within the acceptable range of their expectations are within the ZoT.

For example, if a digital employee expects their laptop to perform a particular task and it does so within the range of their mental "Zone of Tolerance," they're likely satisfied. Scores close to or below the Adequate threshold of the ZoT represent rising dissatisfaction and digital friction.

On the other hand, if the laptop outperforms their ZoT, they now have a new low bar and, presumably, expect superior performance all the time (which is a lose-lose proposition!)

We'll discuss how to find your boundaries and keep digital employee experiences in the zone to optimize productivity, costs, and digital employee experience in Step 6.

4. Disconfirmation Is When We Realize That Our Beliefs Don't Match Reality

Ever wonder what quality of experience you provide to digital employees? Disconfirmation can tell you.

It turns employee expectations and perceptions of IT into actionable insights you need to drive business agility. Adding perception and expectation to Figure I-2 would show the level of satisfaction relative to the upper and lower boundaries of the ZoT. It describes the differences between what digital employees expect and experience.

The difference between what we experience and expect is our disconfirmation score. Disconfirmation has a simple formula, as shown in Figure I-3.

FIGURE I-3. Disconfirmation Formula

$$QoE = Perception - Expectation$$

Figure I-3 shows that QoE can be a positive or negative value. A negative score suggests we've not met employees' expectations. A positive score indicates that we did, as Figure I-4 shows.

Figure I-4 positions user Expectations and Perceptions to complete the ZoT for a given IT solution, workgroup, application, product, service, team, etc.

FIGURE I-4. Zone of Tolerance Showing Positive Satisfaction (aka Positive Disconfirmation)

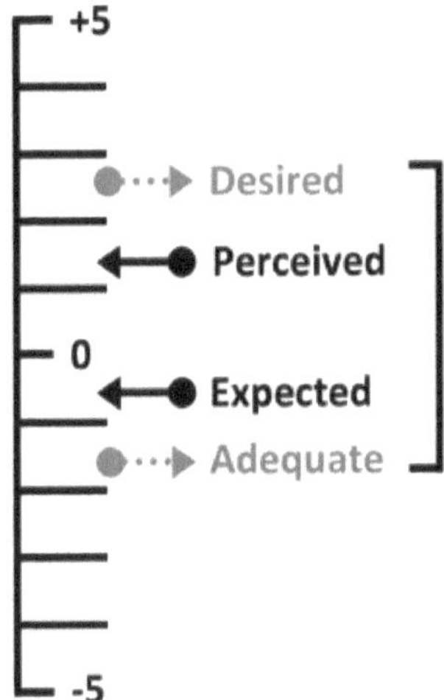

The experience in Figure I-4 is positive because Perceived exceeds Expected (and Adequate) and signals satisfied digital employees. It also shows we're not likely over-spending because Perceived is lower than Desired or the best possible experience.

Focusing on expectations and experiences across the RATER framework to measure employees' feelings about their services and digital workplace solutions, we can identify improvement areas and provide better experiences.

Disconfirmation shows if a consumer is satisfied, delighted, or dissatisfied.

The difference between consumer perceptions and expectations defines satisfaction, and satisfaction over time defines your IT QoE. Its "Q = P-E" formula is the "$E = mc^2$" of IT satisfaction and DEX.

The entire point of any IT quality effort is to satisfy employees or customers during transactions and do so often enough that our consumers think of their experience as high quality.

***

Satisfaction Story: *An IT Satisfaction Survey that Didn't Measure Satisfaction*

Background: I worked with an IT group that built a homemade satisfaction survey they loved because it showed that employees were happy. But employees were dissatisfied with IT and complained to their leadership. As we discussed the results, IT explained that they focused on how well employees liked the technology, its features, and its ease of use. Their explanation surprised me since Tangibles (what the survey asked about) are but one of five factors in satisfaction and often the lowest contributor to dissatisfaction. Unsurprisingly, IT workers thought it was great — they liked it since it confirmed their solution was easy to use, something "everyone knows users need," they told me.

Results: I wasn't surprised by the assumptive attitude or how IT positioned this survey to measure IT satisfaction in a way that made them look good. It explained why the survey only asked about the perception of Tangibles. The root cause of this satisfaction effort's failure was that IT asked the wrong questions and didn't know the expectations held by employees. (Remember, never invent your questions!) Rather than asking about one dimension of satisfaction — the one that made IT look good, they should have asked how the existing solution met or didn't meet employee and customer expectations. For example, they should have asked about the required Reliability, Responsiveness, and the rest of the RATER factors. Better yet, they should have just used CES!

Conclusion: By understanding employee expectations across the RATER spectrum, they could have tailored their digital workplace solutions to employee needs.

***

As an IT leader, it's essential always to know the expectations of your IT consumers and measure overall experience against the ZoT for each RATER determinant, not just single facets of the overall experience (like Tangibles in the preceding Satisfaction Story example.)

Doing so will ensure you create a product or service completely tuned to their needs. You build sustainable IT satisfaction with your employees by analyzing disconfirmation. Step 7 is all about disconfirmation and its essential role in IT satisfaction, diagnosis, and improvement.

5. Your Service Concept Is Your Super Power for Improving Digital Employee Experience

I've found that IT leaders often forget to consider a key factor when making decisions.

One simple omission can lead to a bad experience for digital employees, high staff turnover, and decreased market value.

It's all avoidable if you take the time to consider the impact of IT decisions on your external customers by linking your IT strategy to business value.

Focus on delivering a positive experience to external customers by meeting the needs of internal customers and users.

A service concept is a tool used to identify and define expectations of IT, employee outcomes, and business value — and plan the best way to meet them. It's a document that describes the purpose of an IT solution's goals and objectives, its functionality, business value, and operational environment in business terms.

It's just like a blueprint when building or remodeling your home.

> "Any system or blueprint for success is better than none at all."
>
> —*Brian Tracey*

Similarly, we create service concepts in IT for our solutions as our blueprints for collaboration and alignment to deliver business agility and value from IT investments.

It (almost!) goes without saying that IT requires digital employee experience input to adapt to changing employee requirements, as illustrated in Figure I-5 by the lower dotted line between DEX and IT.

FIGURE I-5. The Relationship Between IT, Employee Experience, and Business Success

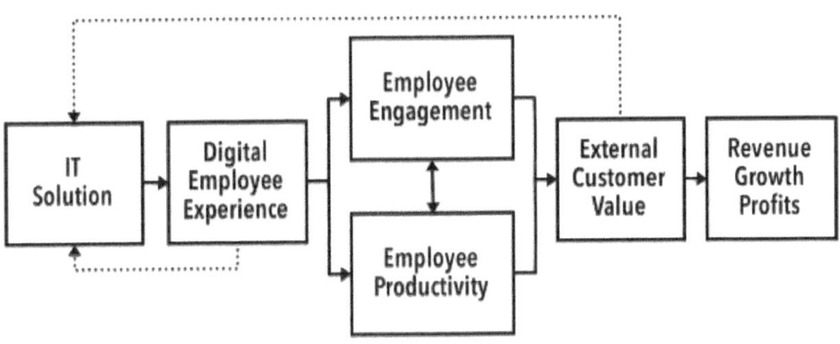

The bidirectional arrows in Figure I-5 signify the integration required for a cohesive and aligned IT service concept. Each component is crucial in ensuring a well-functioning and sustainable (valuable, profitable) IT solution.

What most IT folks miss, however, is the upper dotted line in Figure I-5, representing the addition of external customer value as a critical IT input. This is the missing link, business value — not revenue, profits, or growth.

Why not focus on revenue instead? Because revenue, growth, and profits result from external customer value. Deliver the right IT solution, and profits will follow.

Your service concept is your IT business value proposition.

It's also where we develop an IT solution's BVaR — the value it provides to a workgroup and the company.

> "Business and human endeavors are systems... we tend to focus on snapshots of isolated parts of the system. And wonder why our deepest problems never get solved."
>
> *— Peter Senge*

This value goes beyond simply understanding the cost of the solution. Instead, it looks at the potential impact of the solution not operating as intended regarding business outcomes. The opposite is also true — the impact when the solution works as expected.

BVaR is situational. The same application can have different levels of value by individual, team, and function.

***

Satisfaction Story: *Service Concept "Business Value at Risk"*

Background: The IT organization at a soft drink bottling company had IT "technical debt" that affected its network. The application controlling the bottling assembly line relied on the network, as did many others. IT leaders had requested a $200,000 budget for network equipment upgrades to enhance reliability. IT didn't co-create a service concept because it was hard to engage the business. Thus, they failed to justify the expense in business terms. Since the business had no idea how the network related to the bottling line, they denied the funding request. Consequently, the network experienced multiple failures before addressing the technical debt. Each failure prevented the processing of orders from distributors.

Results: The bottling plant had to shut down six times. Managers stopped production and sent the workers home each time. The losses required overtime to recover. The total cost of these failures was over $2,500,000.

Conclusion: This network application's BVaR was over $900,000 daily to just the bottling line. Had the IT department co-created a service concept, everyone involved would have known about the network application's BVaR. If they had, business leaders could have made a more informed decision and funded the upgrades earlier, avoiding substantial losses.

***

Having a good user experience with IT solutions is vital. Your service concept ensures that IT implementation and business vision are synchronized by outlining how IT should meet these expectations and how they contribute to overall business performance. We'll learn how to create and use service concepts in step 8.

6. Bonus #1! The Gaps Model Shows Where in IT Dissatisfaction Arises

It's common sense that we should always make it simple for our digital employees to do their jobs well.

Focusing on their satisfaction can help our digital employees be more productive and happier, boosting employee retention and profits.

But there's another way to improve the digital experience and provide extra value to our employees, customers, and company: by using the Gaps Model.

FIGURE I-6. The Gaps Model

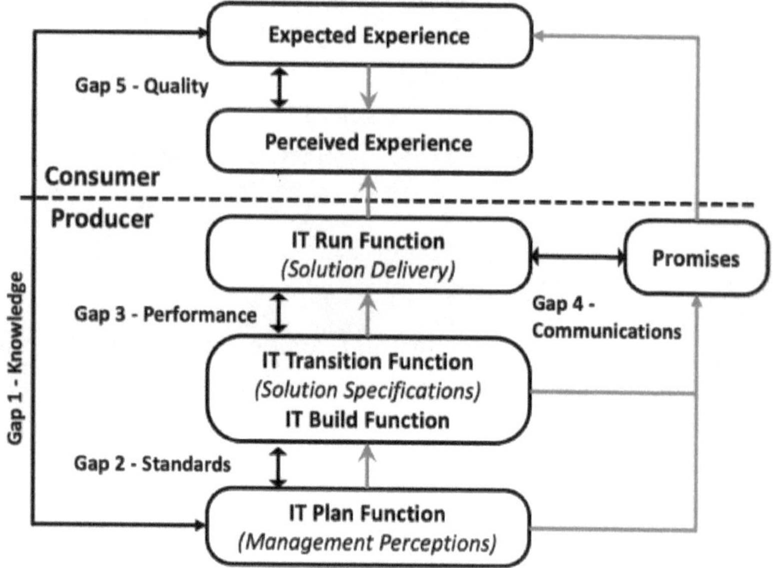

Figure I-6 shows the primary IT functions of planning, building, transitioning, and running (PBTR) and how missteps lead to measurable gaps in solution delivery. This results in IT dissatisfaction at Gap 5 as low QoE.

The Gaps model is the "glue" that binds an IT solution's experience to IT satisfaction. It answers, "Where do missed expectations and IT delivery problems arise?"

It's easy to confuse experience and satisfaction, but they differ. Experience can be positive or negative and is how you feel after interacting with an IT solution or service. Satisfaction is when that experience falls within your expectations. They're related, though, and you can use their relationship to design experience or improve satisfaction.

"90% of all management problems are caused by miscommunication."

—Dale Carnegie

The Gaps Model is the tool that bridges and connects IT work with digital employee experience as measured by IT satisfaction. It explains the root causes of IT failures across the classic IT PBTR functions.

Gaps are optional extensions to measure IT delivery but are indispensable to improving it.

SERVQUAL introduced the Gaps Model, which is unique in its use. It identifies the five gaps in IT solution creation and delivery. If your IT consumers are dissatisfied (Gap 5), it's likely due to Gaps 1 to 4 issues. These gaps represent the different stages of IT production regarding strategy/planning (Gap 1), design/building (Gap 2), delivery/transitioning (Gap 3), and operation/running (Gap 4.)

Using specific guidance for each gap, you can quickly identify and address areas for improvement in solutions and identify likely causes — and solutions — to improve IT satisfaction.

***

Satisfaction Story: *IT Staff Retention with Low Customer Satisfaction*

Background: Customers of a leading worldwide provider of telecommunication services to multinational companies consistently scored low on loyalty measures. IT employees were disengaged and quitting. The surface cause was customers calling service staff directly, skipping the central service desk. Worse, customers asked service delivery employees to work outside their service level agreements. The root cause was that, to close deals, sales staff gave service personnel contact information to customers and said to avoid the IT service desk for the best service.

Results: Sales pressures sabotaged delivery staff and dissatisfied customers by trying to over-deliver. This problem caused unhappy customers and employee churn resulting in a loss of reputation and profits — on a global scale.

Conclusion: Customer contact personnel often face pressure to deliver what the business promises — especially if those promises do not align with internal processes. In this case, employees we're quitting due to stress. The cause of this issue was a Gap 4 problem — a mismatch between promises made and IT delivery. A combination of *Role Stress* (difference between expected and perceived roles), *Role Conflict* (trying to meet incompatible demands), and Role Ambiguity (unclear directions) — in short, a lack of IT leadership!

***

The Gaps model provides a data-driven approach to pinpoint and tackle the root causes of satisfaction issues, making it valuable for enhancing digital employee experience. In step 9, we'll use a case study that shows how to find and fix IT delivery problems once and for all!

7. Bonus #2! Justify IT Projects in Business Outcome Terms

To achieve optimal results, aligning your project with business outcomes is crucial. Speaking the language of business decision-makers (and avoiding the tech jargon!) is essential to secure IT funding and justify improvements.

You must translate IT enhancements into tangible business value using industry-specific terms. Imagine meeting with the CIO or CFO or doing a board presentation for funding an IT project when you read the following Satisfaction Story.

***

Satisfaction Story: *Justifying an IT system upgrade in business terms.*

Background: You work for a technical training company. Technical debt is causing problems that require technical support to resolve. Educators spend about 10,000 hours per year in IT service desk queues and talking with service desk agents. You're asking the executive committee for funding. Following is your dialog.

You: I've identified 10,000 educator hours we can recover. That's the equivalent of roughly three professional trainers. This would improve learner outcomes too. Would you like me to pursue it?

Them: How much?

You: $500,000 over 6 months.

Them: Approved! When can you start?

***

Each IT solution either adds to or detracts from value, with multiple benefits collectively contributing to business value. Identify the value IT improvements bring to your company, such as the educator, learner, and business outcomes in the preceding example, and lead with that.

The goal is to determine business value and effectively communicate it in concise business terms. Step 10 is where I provide an approach and template. You'll learn how to show leadership why your IT satisfaction improvements require funding in a way that works — if not like magic — at least more reliably that leading with technology!

IT Satisfaction Components Share a Relationship

Perceptions set the core functionality of an IT solution and define value in terms of employee results. Expectations represent IT quality in terms of tolerance bands (Zone of Tolerance) for the Reliability, Assurance, Tangibles, Empathy, and Responsiveness determinants, which define the experience you deliver via disconfirmation. They all rely on the Service Concept to link business strategy to your IT solutions — not as a power-user journey map but as a complete view of how you plan to facilitate the results of employees, customers, and your business based on BVaR.

BVaR and the ZoT also change if perceptions or expectations change. When that happens, the Gaps model lets you remediate by extending or reducing RATER levels to keep your delivery "in the zone." These are the new tools in your IT experience satisfaction toolbox.

Used in combination, you will deliver world-class IT solutions to your employees and customers.

Because of their relationships, the order in which you use these 5+2 components is crucial.

Over my career, I've seen teams start with perceptions without looking at disconfirmation and not understanding that everything uses expectations as its base.

When this happens, you've missed desired quality, and the ZoT becomes meaningless.

Likewise, I've seen teams start with RATER values and work backward, trying to engineer a solution without knowing what QoE consumers desire — the result is usually overspending due to over-engineering.

However, sometimes it's the opposite, and you roll out a solution that fails to satisfy your consumers.

When you get it correct, though, it's beautiful! If you've ever been party to a smooth IT rollout, you know how satisfying this is!

Diagnosing IT Quality Failures

As an IT leader, understanding digital employee experience and dissatisfaction is essential for providing quality IT solutions and optimizing IT delivery. The approach I present in Completely Satisfied is a great way to get an empirical look into IT experience so that you can recognize and address any issues in time to respond and adjust.

By studying the principles of perception, expectations, the Zone of Tolerance, disconfirmation, the service concept, the gaps model, and BVaR, you get an in-depth view of IT dissatisfaction and develop solutions to help correct it. To begin the process, look for signs such as low NPS or CES scores that can provide an initial indication of quality failures.

Once you've identified these signs, RATER's diagnostic disconfirmation approach helps you pinpoint the cause of the dissatisfaction and localize any underlying issues. Use gap analysis to find where things went wrong in IT and set up your remediation. Finally, you can develop an action plan or QIP (Quality Improvement Plan) to restore IT satisfaction.

In my work with IT organizations large and small, I've found it's vital to use a consistent approach. The workflow I advise you to follow looks like that shown in Figure I-7.

FIGURE I-7. The 5+2 Components of IT Satisfaction

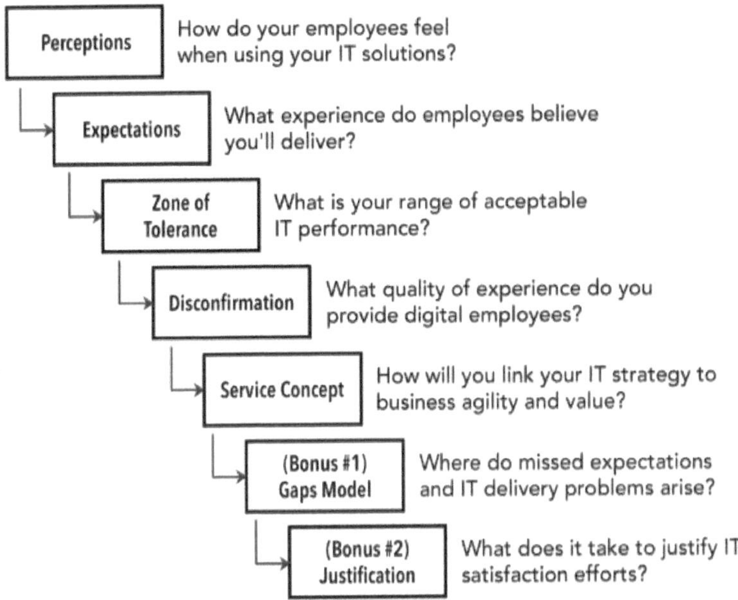

A focused approach like that shown in Figure I-7 will enhance IT delivery efficiency by controlling costs and improving productivity, engagement, and profits. In Part II, I'll provide you with the process for working with the components in the proper order.

Pulling Experience Satisfaction Together

Now that you understand each component of experience satisfaction, you must adapt them to your organization, services, employees, and customers. Are you ready to learn the 10-step experience satisfaction process? I bet you are!

THE 10-STEP EXPERIENCE SATISFACTION PROCESS

STEP 1. LEARN TO LOVE EMPLOYEES WHO HATE YOUR IT SOLUTIONS

When I began working on an actionable approach to improving IT satisfaction, one of the first issues I had to solve was how its components meshed.

Our best targets for satisfaction improvement often depend on knowing three items:

1. Who is least satisfied with an IT solution.
2. The business value we can help them deliver.
3. How to relate that value in business terms to gain their support.

The value we provide depends upon removing digital friction by optimizing our users' digital experiences with IT solutions. But that depends upon business revenues and profits, which requires loyal marketplace customers.

However, that only comes from high levels of quality compared to expectations, as reflected by high employee productivity, but that only comes from a great digital employee experience. When everything depends on everything else, where do we start?

In this step, I'll answer that question. I found my answer by brainstorming with a couple of friends, who, like me, realize that today's IT organization fundamentally differs from every other IT function of the past. That's because virtually every single dollar of business revenue today depends upon information technology.

FIGURE 1-1. The Relationship Between IT Satisfaction and Business Profit

Figure 1-1, inspired by Heskett's "Quality Wheel," shows IT satisfaction's cyclical nature, origins, and outputs. It all starts with great digital employee experience — the source of corporate profits.

Our approaches were similar in that we spent all of our time looking for things that worked and then applying those to improve satisfaction. Which IT customers were happiest? Which features did digital employees enjoy the most? What workgroups had the highest satisfaction ratings?

We kept looking for why some were satisfied, and others weren't — and we did it primarily by talking to the most satisfied IT users and customers. That's when we realized we were doing it backward. Unlike in marketing, for example, we realized that finding satisfied users and trying to convince others that they should or could be happy with just a little training or perhaps some motivation would never work for IT.

Instead, we had to focus on those digital employees that struggled with our digital workplace solutions. We needed to dig into why our IT products and services were hindering rather than helping. We realized we needed to focus on our least satisfied digital employees.

This difference in our perspective was profound.

Harnessing your unhappy employees' insights could unlock the perfect IT solution!

Your most dissatisfied employees can hold the keys to understanding what your IT solution must include. How will you link business agility to IT strategy? By starting with the employees who have the most problems.

We had the tip of the satisfaction iceberg upside down. As soon as we got it right side up, we realized we had to focus on providing a great digital employee experience by seeking out those who were dissatisfied and understanding why.

Much like a canary in the coal mine, dissatisfied digital employees often push the envelope because they work with the most demanding end-customers and face the most challenging business situations. These digital employees can be your richest source of IT improvement opportunities.

Even though I had tried to seek out dissatisfaction by talking to our most satisfied customers (something that I admit sounds dumb in hindsight), we still had to adjust our solutions to meet the needs and expectations of all our employees.

Once we started running satisfaction studies focused on the dissatisfied and began engaging them, we began to spot patterns. Don't get me wrong, those who are satisfied are important, but assuming you're accurately measuring satisfaction, they're not struggling to succeed using the IT kit you provide (though they often have ideas to help too!)

> "You miss 100% of the shots you don't take."
>
> — *Wayne Gretzky*

It's often the most dissatisfied digital employees who know what it takes to satisfy their end-customers in the marketplace. Always remember they're closest to the results that keep your company in business. If they're dissatisfied, the digital workplace solution you've provided probably holds them back. What they're struggling with is what you must understand to be successful.

Another excellent source of this type of IT satisfaction data is customer complaints, so try to solicit them, too!

You'll improve satisfaction faster by concentrating on your worst-fit digital employees.

Employees talk to each other. A dissatisfied employee spreads poor word of mouth about your solution, which can tip other employees. Satisfying these unhappy employees turns them into evangelists for IT, and positive word of mouth helps other employees trust IT more.

So simple to say, but often masked by the complexity of IT systems and multiplied by the size of an organization. However, the adage remains true, "The best way to solve a problem is to tackle it bit by bit, one step at a time."

And so, choosing one IT service, solution, product, customer, business unit, etc., and then gaining competency is what must happen. Not so hard after all, it turns out. It just takes your leadership intensity.

The first step in satisfaction exercises is to list your most unhappy customers and employees.

For example, find experienced employees with a track record of success who are now complaining. Look for those who offer to help you, and listen to them and their supervisors. The insights these digital employees can provide you are just what you need to improve IT satisfaction.

First, they understand the business and have been successful. Secondly, they still care enough to complain to you. Unfortunately, when people stop complaining, it's likely too late.

What if I don't have any engaged but miserable digital employees?

To improve IT satisfaction, you need to have enough dissatisfied employees to spot digital friction patterns and identify one or more targets for improvement. You can take this little test to help. Assuming you're collecting IT satisfaction in a representative and meaningful way, segment your responses by satisfied and dissatisfied.

Next, sort the dissatisfied by their tenure. Do new employees like your IT solutions better than employees who have been there for a while? Do some business groups have a higher percentage of satisfied or dissatisfied users than others? Do the least satisfied share everyday situations or characteristics?

Remember not to assume you already know who or whom you should or shouldn't listen to. Also, be sure you're looking at unfiltered, genuine results, not summaries produced by someone else and cascaded up to you. (That's a frequent Gap 1 fault, by the way!)

Think of your IT satisfaction survey as a magnet on a string that you drag along the beach without knowing what you'll attract. But you know it'll be something ferromagnetic! Whatever "sticks to your magnet," in this analogy, is valuable and represents the digital employees you're trying to find, interview, and learn from.

But I want to start with IT, not pesky digital employees!

Most IT people want to start with technology. And, of course, that makes perfect sense for most of us. An interest in technology brought most of us into IT in the first place. For many of us, it's what we enjoy. It's also a pitfall and the downfall of many.

If you start focusing on technology, you'll start thinking about speeds and feeds, uptime, packet loss, disk space, more tools, and all the other typical IT operational metrics. While those metrics are essential for QoS, they won't solve your QoE problems.

Instead, keep in mind that improving IT satisfaction for digital employees must center on the digital employee point of view, which isn't technological. It's business results-oriented, so think BVaR.

Shouldn't we do what customers want instead of listening to digital employees?

In short, NO! As we'll see later in step 3, customer and user roles aren't the same. They have very different points of view and need unique treatments. If careless, you can lower digital employee experience and satisfaction and even unnecessarily raise the bar.

It's well-known and generally accepted that most leaders have, at best, a vague idea of what their people do daily. We think we know, but many times we're off base. Sure, customers like the SVP of Marketing understand that their marketing teams are doing marketing tasks.

Still, the SVP of marketing isn't interacting with the same tools under the same conditions as someone on their team who works to create and publish ads. That's the critical insight about customers and their users — they're related but have significantly different perspectives.

The SVP of Marketing might hear grumblings from their staff, but they may not have experienced the friction themselves. They're understanding is often diffuse and focused on different problems.

For example, the SVP cares about launching the new $6 million campaign to prepare for the shopping holidays. But their Digital Marketing Specialist is struggling with your digital workplace solution because it won't attach or send appropriately formatted files. These are very different perspectives.

One of these views (user) can help you find and remove digital friction; the other can only feel pain and increase the pressure on IT to do something. You need to focus on the former and calm the latter.

I designed this book and its unique approach to improving satisfaction by working with users — because those digital employees who are contact employees know firsthand what achieving business results requires. They are the only ones who can tell you exactly why your digital workplace solution isn't working for them — which is precisely what you must fix!

Am I measuring IT, a solution, or a feature? Or what?

Along with the conversation around customers and users, we must distinguish between IT (the functional organization) and a specific IT solution composed of products and services.

Most companies have many IT solutions. Usually, there are function-specific IT solutions — for example, sales, marketing, research, support, etc. And then, there is the overall IT organization. The two are related, but they're pretty different.

People can be delighted with an IT solution and dissatisfied with the overall IT organization, as you saw from the previous example of my Internet company.

Now and then, I get asked if we shouldn't start with overall IT satisfaction and then try to find out about a product or service. My answer always depends on how much data you have already collected.

If you've already got statistically significant IT satisfaction surveys, you've probably got the data to drill down into specific services, applications, and digital workplace solutions.

On the other hand, many IT organizations already know which IT solutions are most problematic because they take many complaints and trouble tickets at the IT service desk.

If you've already identified a problem, then that's the place to start. If you haven't, you need to validate your satisfaction survey and begin attracting dissatisfied digital employee users, as I discussed earlier.

Often, it's helpful to speak with customers (especially the leaders of contact personnel) because they're almost as close to the problem as the direct contact employees.

The IT satisfaction approach outlined in this book is helpful for any IT scenario at any level: IT, customer, user, digital employee, or solution feature. Generally speaking, throughout this book, I assume you're working with a specific digital workplace solution and its digital employees, e.g., users. However, you must adjust if you're working at the customer or IT level.

***

Satisfaction Story: *Dissatisfaction Leads to Digital Transformation*

Background: A large healthcare provider faced challenges with its digital employee experience after implementing a new Service Desk self-service solution. Employees found it challenging to use the system and didn't engage with it as intended. The IT leader set out to enhance IT satisfaction by identifying dissatisfied employees and determining the self-service portals BVaR — the cost of not addressing their needs through self-service. It was unclear if the self-service portal project's primary goal was to reduce IT workload or improve employee productivity.

Results: IT surveyed users using the RATER framework to identify the least satisfied employees and those with the most tenure. Subsequently, they prioritized the results based on BVaR determined as clinician time spent in the queue and on hold. Interestingly, the findings revealed that employees new to the Service Desk were the least satisfied, while those with more experience were the most satisfied. Dissatisfied employees highlighted areas where addressing their issues could deliver business value, including enhanced collaboration and communication, training, and improved data security.

Conclusion: The company prioritized areas with the most significant impact on employee satisfaction and business value by identifying the least satisfied employees and recognizing the potential business value from addressing their concerns. IT was able to return thousands of clinician hours to the business, improving healthcare delivery for their community.

***

Dissatisfaction is the key to IT satisfaction and your success!

In step 1, we learned the value of IT dissatisfaction. Let's continue to the next chapter on forming a satisfaction team. This team will help identify improvement areas and ensure employees receive the best solutions possible.

STEP 2. FORM A SATISFACTION TEAM

Nurturing digital employee experience requires IT, employee, and business collaboration. Each party has distinct expectations, views, and values, so guiding them in discovering new opportunities to work together is paramount to your success.

Forming a Satisfaction Team to improve digital employee experience provides the necessary insights to remove digital friction to enhance experience, engagement, productivity, and profits.

Your first meeting with this team has to bring all those insights to the surface by working through a service concept conversation. Discussing the service concept is a "safe topic" and gets everyone on the same page.

In this step, we'll discuss what this team has to do and how they must work together.

Digital Employee Experience Enhancement Team

Improving IT satisfaction is a business problem requiring IT and business collaboration. By forming a diverse and empowered Satisfaction Team, you can work together to identify issues and find solutions to shared productivity problems.

IT satisfaction isn't an IT problem; it's a business problem.

More than once, clients asked me why IT can't go it alone and make the necessary changes to improve digital employee experience. My answer is straightforward — this isn't an IT problem to solve. If IT alone could have solved it, we wouldn't have a problem, would we?

Here's why improving IT satisfaction is a business problem that takes a team composed of IT producers and consumers to fix. (Hint, see Figure I-5 again!) IT leaders and workers need the business view because this is how digital employee experience problems progress:

- Business employees are the first to feel the pain of IT solutions with low QoE.
- End-customers in your marketplace are next to feel this pain because contact personnel cannot meet end-customer requirements.
- Marketing detects negative word of mouth and falling brand loyalty.
- Sales start experiencing end-customer churn and longer revenue cycles.
- Human Resources feels it next as employee retention and recruiting problems.
- Business leaders and shareholders take notice as profits drop.

IT satisfaction is a business problem we can only solve together. Only as prosumers can we improve IT satisfaction, employee productivity, end-customer satisfaction, business agility, and results like profits and growth. We must work together because each requires the other to be successful, and each has unique insights into satisfaction.

"Seek first to understand, then to be understood."

— *Stephen Covey*

Job #1 for your prosumer Satisfaction Team is perceptual and experiential diversity.

Delivering a great digital employee experience takes a team of IT and business customers and users. All must work together as prosumers because each requires the other to be successful, and each has unique insights into the contributors and detractors of satisfaction.

When forming a cross-functional prosumer team to improve IT satisfaction, it's common to discover that team members have different perceptions and understandings of what satisfaction is, does, how it originates, and how to resolve it.

Since your goal is to improve IT satisfaction by collaboratively focusing on experience for a given IT solution, it's important to air and level-set core terms and concepts in your first meeting and every meeting with a new prosumer team member. The 5+2 waterfall diagram is a great job aid — see Figure I-7. I've got other job aids available at hankmarquis.com.

The Satisfaction Team, responsible for improving digital employee experience, will have several key responsibilities. By fulfilling these responsibilities, the Satisfaction Team aims to remove digital friction, improve digital employee experience, enhance engagement, boost productivity, and ultimately drive profits and growth for the organization.

The job of your Satisfaction Team includes:

- **Leading the service concept conversation.** The team will initiate and facilitate an IT service concept conversation. They'll work together to discuss and define the core terms, concepts, and IT satisfaction expectations. This conversation helps align team members' understanding and ensures everyone is on the same page. We'll get into the service concept in detail in Step 8.
- **Identifying contributors and engaging detractors.** The team will collaboratively identify the factors contributing to or detracting from IT satisfaction. Activities here include analyzing IT solutions, infrastructure, architecture, applications, processes, client success, sales, and other relevant business areas. They will explore employee and end-customer experiences and pain points to understand satisfaction drivers better. The team must represent customer and user goals — they are not always the same!
- **Empowering agile problem resolution by taking immediate action.** As issues and challenges related to IT satisfaction surface, the team will take ownership of problem resolution. With an empowered IT executive leading the team, they can address and solve problems quickly. This ability to take immediate action makes the team credible, as it enhances the team's agility and ensures that issues identified get addressed.
- **Facilitating collaborative alignment by bridging IT and**

Business for enhanced satisfaction. The team will foster collaboration and alignment between IT and the business. They'll bridge the gap between IT solutions and their impact on the company. By involving representatives from each IT function and working closely with stakeholders from the business side, the team will ensure that improvements in IT satisfaction positively impact business agility, profits, and end-customer retention.

- **Promoting continuous improvement by enhancing digital employee experience.** The Satisfaction Team will drive ongoing IT satisfaction efforts. They will implement strategies, processes, and initiatives to improve digital employee experience. The team must gather feedback, measure satisfaction levels, implement or recommend necessary changes, and monitor the impact of those changes over time.

Leading the Digital Employee Experience Enhancement Team

Improving IT satisfaction impacts business agility, profits, and end-customer retention directly. IT cannot and should not attempt this alone. A senior IT leader must own and run the meeting. In smaller firms, this could be the CIO or CTO. In larger firms, this person might be a Sr. Director, VP, or even an IT Product Owner in more progressive IT organizations.

Why an IT leader and not a business leader? Because although the results of the changes will primarily affect the business, the changes will be mainly within IT, not the business.

Why this level of leadership? Because the cross-functional nature of prosumer teams requires the level of authority to solve any problems the team raises on the spot.

Who should be on the Satisfaction Team?

Along with an empowered IT executive, team members depend on the scope of the IT satisfaction effort.

Ideally, the team should include the IT producer and consumer group members for a given IT solution. Complete representation is critical since each IT section, from infrastructure to architecture to applications and client success to sales, has unique insight into the contributors and detractors of their digital employee experiences.

One type of individual to avoid, however, is the so-called Superuser. They're not representative of the majority of users. What Superusers consider normal is often impossible for average workers. By definition, Superusers are already operating at the pinnacle.

Sure, collect information from them, but spend most of your time with ordinary users who struggle to succeed.

IT solutions need a full house.

You need face-to-face representation from each IT function because IT solution delivery is end-to-end, not piecemeal. You want team representatives who "do the work" and those who lead. But you don't want people who take notes for others or too many people altogether, or nothing gets accomplished.

In team sports, a basketball team needs five players, baseball nine, and soccer eleven. There are psychological reasons for those odd numbers which are not obvious (and measuring satisfaction is a psychometric function!)

Here are some insights about team sizes. Teams with:

- More than five members interact less per member, and members tend to form cliques (five appears to link to the natural limits of our short-term memory.)
- Fifteen or fewer members tend to bond (fifteen appears to be our natural level of deep trust, such as loved ones vs. friends vs. acquaintances.)
- An even number of members can deadlock.
- Twenty or more members tend to get less accomplished because we naturally digress into subgroups and struggle to reach a consensus.

A good IT Satisfaction Team could have an odd number of people (maybe 5 or 9), and 15 might be your maximum productive team size.

You're now informed about team sizes but use common sense too. With some guardrails around adequate team size, your next step is to select representatives from each party represented in your service concept.

Lead the IT satisfaction charge!

Who should lead the satisfaction exercise? I have run hundreds of IT improvement workshops over my career. I get invited in most of the time because the internal leader isn't getting the desired results from their team. It can also be challenging for an internal person to be able to speak truth to power. Most internal people share the same perspective, too, so it's challenging to think about new ways of doing things.

Bringing in an experienced outsider opens up new opportunities and removes limitations on the facilitator. Having someone outside the company to facilitate the discussion will make the IT satisfaction exercise much more productive and balanced. You will get to value much sooner with someone who is only vested in your successful outcome and knows how to do that in the best way possible.

It takes a village to enhance digital employee experience.

Collaboration between IT and business professionals, led by an IT executive, is crucial for enhancing digital employee experience and driving positive outcomes. Co-creating requires a Satisfaction Team to ensure digital employee experience is satisfactory.

With members from IT and business backgrounds, their different perspectives will help them spot problems, fix them, and work together.

The team will also talk about the service given, pay attention to the user experience, find people who can help and those who might be unhelpful, help solve problems efficiently, make sure everyone agrees or at least understands tradeoffs, and keep trying to improve.

By having an IT executive in charge, they can take action quickly, leading to better satisfaction and outcomes.

Getting serious about IT satisfaction and digital employee experience.

The Satisfaction Team needs a repository, a tool to capture and track IT improvements. At the most extreme, there are detailed standards for complaints handling, such as the ISO 10001 (Code of Conduct), 10002 (Complaint Handling), 10003 (Dispute Resolution), and 10004 standards (Customer Satisfaction). They represent everything you might need but can be too much for many, including new IT Satisfaction Teams. At the other extreme, you could use a simple spreadsheet too.

Either way or somewhere in between, you need to manage the process of improving digital employee experience and managing the data you will collect from your IT satisfaction exercises.

The technical term for this tool is a Solution/Service Quality Information System (SQIS.) What you need to track varies. The types of data collection can include:

- **Transactional surveys** are measured after an encounter to get feedback while the experience is fresh and act quickly if needed, with continuous frequency; however, the limitation is that it is a point-in-time measure and does not represent Quality of Experience (QoE).
- **Exit interviews** to determine why employees leave specifically to assess the role of IT in loyalty, with a continuous frequency and the limitation of requiring knowledge of employee IT solutions.
- **Focus groups** are a way to survey a specific IT topic with a small group of 8 to 12 users or customers to provide informal feedback and solicit improvements. However, it should be used cautiously to avoid suppressing potential negative feedback.

- **An advisory panel** that provides quarterly feedback and advice to gain in-depth feedback and suggestions about IT performance. Be aware that Superuser feedback is irrelevant for most "average users."
- **IT Solution reviews** involve periodic visits with a class of consumers to discuss and assess their relationship, a future-focused face-to-face identification of expectations, performance perception, and improvement priorities that should be done annually or semiannually. It can be time-consuming for both parties, but it's well worth it.
- **User complaints** require categorization, tracking, and sharing to identify common failures continuously. One limitation of this approach is that dissatisfied users often don't complain, skewing your data.
- **Operational QoS data** that is captured, categorized, tracked, and reported. However, QoS data doesn't always align with perceptions of satisfaction.

I recommend starting where you are with what you've got. My simple guidance to clients is as follows:

- Use your existing ITSM ticketing or support tool. If a customer or user complains, capture it as an Incident in your ticketing tool, perhaps ServiceNow.
- If your team finds a pattern, open a Problem. Your IT Satisfaction Team are your "satisfaction troubleshooters" and will be responsible for solving the issue.
- Be sure to capture all the learning via your tools Knowledge Management facilities and communicate with affected stakeholders using its messaging features.

In this step, we built a working IT satisfaction team. Now you're ready for ways to measure and track IT satisfaction to ensure it keeps getting better!

STEP 3. RALLY YOUR TEAM AROUND THE LANGUAGE OF SATISFACTION

When seeking to improve digital employee experience, the old ways we know best are no longer helpful.

IT complexity multiplied by business model decisions equals a unique environment. You and your team are probably experts in talking about technology. If you're like most, your teams probably have their own "IT dialect" and struggle to reach common ground.

By the time we get to talking about the business, we often have trouble communicating. Not just talking to each other, but especially when talking to customers and users. To lead IT successfully, you must deliberately change your perspective to understand your IT solution as your consumers do. That requires a shared "satisfaction vocabulary."

As you saw from my discussion about internal and external customers and users, words genuinely matter to achieving consensus in improving IT satisfaction. You've probably experienced situations where IT teams had trouble working together because they used different terminology to describe shared IT activities. I learned this firsthand too. Earlier in my career, one department referred to an IT change as a "release," while another called it a "deployment." That's three terms, two of which mean different things in different contexts.

I learned that not having a common vocabulary led to confusion and inconsistencies. The absence of a common way to talk about digital employee experience made analyzing data, identifying issues, and proposing solutions difficult.

It hindered our communication and kept us arguing instead of expressing our ideas and opinions clearly. We found it challenging to understand each other, and our IT consumers (internal and external) suffered.

I'll explain how to solve common IT satisfaction miscommunication issues in this step.

Harmonize your team by orchestrating a shared lexicon for IT satisfaction.

Align your experience management vocabulary around defined and shared terms for shared experiences. Improving IT satisfaction is a team effort, and all team members must have a shared vocabulary that accurately represents the issues, activities, and solutions for managing IT satisfaction and improving employee experience. This shared language helps ensure everyone is on the same page and can communicate effectively, reducing misunderstandings and delays.

If you've been lucky enough to pull the team together, the last thing you want is to have created a tower of babel. Nothing is worse than watching a critically important meeting degenerate into arguing over semantics and definitions or misunderstanding and misconstruing what someone is trying to say because of terminology.

The assembled team must then align regarding the following IT lexicon terms:

- IT solutions are varied and include names like product, service, tool, application, digital workplace, SaaS, kit, etc.
- The roles of IT satisfaction improvement, distinctions between internal and external users and customers.
- What satisfaction means to whom, why it's essential, and how people's perspectives differ on the same topic — and why that's imperative to success.
- Which components make up satisfaction, and how to define each, their role, and sequencing.
- How IT and business terminology impacts co-creation and our approaches to improve digital employee experience and IT satisfaction.
- QoE vs. QoS and their critical importance and distinctions to IT success.

"There is the strange power we have of changing facts by the force of the imagination."

— *Virginia Woolf*

The preceding points' depth reinforces this step's importance: you need a concise vocabulary to improve IT satisfaction. Just consider how often we in IT confuse the most fundamental roles of "customer" and "user," for example. It worsens when you think about internal or external "customers" and "users," too. And what about the relationship between those roles? Those terms aren't optimal, but they're the default lexicon of IT and business. Yet they make us add extra context and complexity to our conversations.

In my workshops, we review IT satisfaction concepts for the first hour or so. I show Figure 3-1 during this conversation to illustrate the clarity and precision needed to solve IT satisfaction problems. I reinforce that we must all use the same words and terms because we'll get better results and deliver more value to our organizations and consumers when we do.

FIGURE 3-1. The IT View of Customer and User Roles

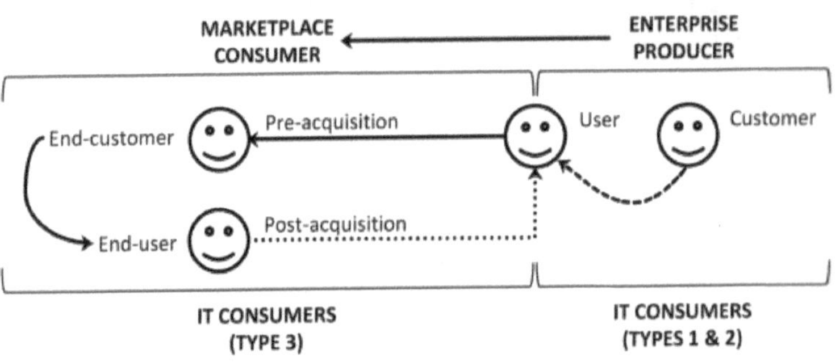

In Figure 3-1, I break down the internal and external roles affected by IT solutions, but the combinations can get even more confusing. The types or classes of delivery (1, 2, and 3) are important distinctions to consider. Each class has specific situations and obstacles to overcome when managing their IT operations based on value.

1. **Marketplace Consumer** refers to people external to an enterprise. External to the enterprise, these folks may or may not consume IT solutions directly.
2. **Enterprise Producer** is an IT organization, one or more of three types: Type 1 is an IT organization serving a business unit within an enterprise. Type 2 IT organizations deliver to

the entire enterprise. Type 3 offers IT solutions directly to an external marketplace.

3. **Customer** is an internal company role specifying requirements for enterprise IT solutions (products and services) for a business function. For example, the SVP of Sales in your company probably decided to go with Salesforce.com or not.

4. **User** is an internal role that employs the IT solution (like Salesforce) selected by a customer to perform daily activities on behalf of an enterprise (like selling and servicing.) The user is the role that interacts with your external marketplace of end-users and end-customers. Users also engage with internal employees in user or customer roles — for example, a benefits administrator in Human Resources is a user of your HRM solution and works with other employees.

5. **End-Customer** is a role external to your company that specifies the requirements for buying or obtaining whatever your company sells or provides. Perhaps your company sells industrial robots. The person purchasing the industrial robots for their company is typically not the same person who will program them. That would be the end-user.

6. **End-User** is the role that consumes the products or services your users (employees) sell or provide to end-customers.

But wait — there's one more thing! Digital employees are stakeholders who can be consumers, providers, users, or customers — sometimes more than one at a time -- as long as they're internal. (We'll leave out contractors to keep things simple!)

Sometimes, they're contact employees or those in customer service, sales, engineering, or other roles that involve interacting with external end-customers and end-users. While we're at it, a consumer is any internal or external user or customer (including machines and AI) that employs or interacts with our IT solutions (I bet you never thought about application developers as users, but they are!)

And producers are the solution providers, typically IT, but not always. Think about Cisco WebEx. IT sets some of its parameters but Cisco hosts and delivers the application.

Here are some other simple everyday examples:

- Our end-customers and end-users see our entire enterprise as the producer of whatever you sell or do.
- Employees in a customer role can also be a user.
- Did you realize that the CIO is often an IT customer and user?
- IT service desk agents are users of the IT service management tool you provided.
- Some end-customers become end-users after they purchase, while others don't.
- While you may integrate your CRM solution, the actual producer of Salesforce.com isn't IT!

All this means is that words matter, and being precise matters. Don't fixate, but be aware of the context; it's crucial. In this book, I use the terms in Figure 3-1.

The reality is that IT consumers see IT solutions as a means to an end.

It's no longer enough for IT providers to think of their solutions as separate bits and pieces (if it ever was.) IT consumers see your IT solution as a holistic solution that addresses their needs. They don't see their digital workplace solution as a collection of cloud storage, network security, and data analytics. Nor do they see it as an integrated solution tailored to their unique needs and requirements. They see it as their job. It pays their bills and feeds their family.

The challenge we face as IT leaders is to understand the needs of our consumers and provide a comprehensive solution that meets those needs. By understanding the specific needs of our consumers, we can customize our solutions to meet their needs.

Examples could include:

- Changing performance profiles for users who work with premium end-customers.
- Offering tailored training materials.
- Bumping up reliability by moving a maintenance window.
- Customizing the interface.
- Providing personalized support.

Finally, we must also be willing to adapt to the changing needs of our consumers.

As user requirements continue to evolve, IT providers must be able to adjust their solutions to keep up.

For example, developing new or deprecating old or duplicate features, updating existing components, overhauling self-help articles, and simplifying workflows.

Dissatisfaction starts with our disconnect between understanding an IT solution as its provider and understanding it as our digital employees perceive it.

Our digital employees may find it challenging even though we provide a solution that meets all the technical requirements. In such cases, we may not have considered the user experience when creating our solution, leading to frustration and dissatisfaction.

To ensure that IT solutions are successful, organizations must bridge the gap between understanding an IT solution from the provider's and the digital employee's points of view. It's essential to understand the needs of the digital employee and create a solution that provides a positive user experience, as it helps accomplish core business results and minimizes BVaR.

Do you know the vocabulary of your users? By learning to speak the same language as IT users and our peers, we can understand how to meet our business needs best.

These steps ensure that our IT solutions are successful and that our digital employees are satisfied.

***

Satisfaction Story: *Profits Lost for Want of a Shared Language*

Background: The company, a technology consulting firm, had IT satisfaction trouble even though it had invested in IT to accommodate an expanding workforce and digital projects. Challenges with resolving IT problems showed up in the form of low satisfaction scores. The IT department had different ways of referring to which aspects of delivery did what, leading to chaos and slowing problem resolution. They also confused internal and external customers. Without a standard language, it was tough for IT teams to work together correctly, making things inefficient and slowing down productivity. Moreover, having no consistent terms meant data quality was poor, so assessing the situation and making sensible decisions was harder.

Results: IT created a vocabulary list based on RATER. With RATER quality of experience terms, communication between IT teams was more straightforward, cut down on misunderstandings, and sped up problem-solving. It also broke down knowledge boundaries, encouraged collaboration, and improved data accuracy.

Conclusion: Implementing a common IT language boosted productivity, reduced downtime, and made employees happier. It also saved money and made it easier to make decisions, resulting in better outcomes for the company.

***

To establish a shared satisfaction vocabulary based on the principles outlined in Completely Satisfied, you can take these actions:

1. **Define key terms:** Start by identifying the key terms and concepts related to IT satisfaction and digital employee experience, as suggested in this book. Determine the definitions of these terms based on their relevance to your organization and the specific context of your IT solutions.

2. **Conduct workshops or training sessions:** Organize workshops incorporating "Completely Satisfied" teachings to align the team members' understanding of the shared vocabulary. Encourage team members to read relevant book sections to deepen their knowledge and facilitate productive discussions.

3. **Establish standardized language:** Encourage the consistent

use of the shared vocabulary outlined here during team discussions, meetings, and documentation. Emphasize the importance of aligning terminology to ensure effective communication.

4. **Encourage feedback and iteration:** Foster an environment where team members can provide feedback on the shared vocabulary, drawing from their understanding of IT satisfaction. Encourage discussions to evaluate the effectiveness of the shared vocabulary and explore potential refinements or additions. Maintain an open dialogue to improve and refine the shared language continuously.

5. **Reinforce and review:** Regularly reinforce the use of the shared vocabulary rooted in the principles of IT satisfaction during team interactions and discussions. Continuously assess the relevance and applicability of the shared terminology, considering updates or adjustments as needed based on insights from this book.

Dropping IT perception biases.

The goal of the 10-step satisfaction process is to find the most impactful issue for an IT solution with the highest BVaR and resolve it using a repeatable and sustainable approach.

But IT folks usually consider IT a collection of technology and find it hard to see or describe it any other way. In this step, we focused on shifting our perspectives through our vocabulary.

By following this advice and referencing these pages as a foundational resource, you can create a shared satisfaction vocabulary that aligns with the principles and teachings outlined in this book. This approach promotes effective communication, collaboration, and understanding among team members, further enhancing the improvement efforts related to IT satisfaction and digital employee experience.

About now, people in workshops ask, "When will we get into measuring satisfaction?" The next chapter is your answer!

STEP 4. UNDERSTAND YOUR IT SATISFACTION OPTIONS

Our business customers and digital employees don't always see IT solutions the way we in IT do, but their perception is all that matters.

It's only natural for us in IT to feel a sense of pride in the solutions we produce since we designed, built, delivered, and operate them. And that's a problem. You need to realize that you don't use the solutions you provide as your digital employees do.

In this step, we'll see the criticality of understanding, appreciating, and accepting that their point of view, even when it isn't flattering to us, is all that matters. We'll answer the question, How do your employees feel when using your IT solutions?

IT satisfaction improvement centers on what digital employees feel makes them most successful, as reflected by what they cannot do.

A key indicator of business success is the satisfaction of digital employees with IT. It's our job to help them market, sell, manufacture, deliver, and support what our business offers. However, IT satisfaction isn't always easy to achieve. To truly improve IT satisfaction levels, you must understand what makes digital employees feel successful.

One approach is focusing on what digital employees cannot do. In other words, the obstacles that prevent them from achieving their goals using our IT solutions. Identifying these obstacles can help us implement changes that make digital employees more successful.

Perception refers to a subjective evaluation of your IT solution by its consumers. We improve IT satisfaction and enhance our company's productivity by addressing their perceived pain points. You're probably wondering, "So, how do we measure perception?" The answer is that you probably already are!

You're off to a great start if you're using CES or NPS. If you're using Kano-derived CSAT or other methods of asking your IT customers and users if they're satisfied, you're trying. But you're probably not measuring their perception of IT in a way that helps you improve.

In the first two cases, you're likely measuring their satisfaction with a transaction. Satisfaction is a judgment of a specific transaction or encounter, but QoE is satisfaction over time. Those two very different activities are not directly equivalent.

To improve IT satisfaction (their perception), you must first improve QoE (their experience) as measured by the five RATER factors.

Breaking down the contenders: NPS vs. CES.

In the red corner, weighing in with a Net Promoter Score of up to 100, it's the heavyweight champion, NPS! And in the blue corner, with a Customer Effort Score that packs a punch, weighing in with a maximum score of 7, it's the challenger, CES! Get ready for a showdown as we break down the differences between these two champions to see which one comes out on top in the battle for loyalty.

All kidding aside, CES, and especially NPS, tend to inspire intense emotional commitment because they are:

- Relatively easy to use,
- Cheap (as in free),
- Fairly accurate at predicting loyalty (but not experience, which we already discussed!)

While they measure loyalty, NPS relies on the idea that you must be satisfied if you feel loyal to a brand. Meanwhile, CES assumes you must be satisfied if your recovery transaction went well. Of course, these assumptions are only sometimes valid.

For example, you can be highly dissatisfied with your Internet provider because they have many outages. At the same time, you can be delighted with their repair person who gets your service working again without getting your carpet dirty.

While you can often recover from a poor IT encounter or transaction, if you can't meet expectations consistently, you've got a real problem. It takes meeting expectations over time — sustained satisfaction — to deliver a quality experience as an effective IT organization.

The CES vs. NPS problem.

CES and NPS focus on transactions, not QoE. According to their owners, these tools' goals are commercial (end-customer) success in terms of loyalty. What could go wrong if you ask your employees if they're satisfied using a one-line question designed to assess end-customer future purchase intent?

One example of what could go wrong if you focus on maximizing satisfaction after a transaction is that it can create a distorted picture, suggesting that employees are either more or less happy than they are. Many of us see this reflected in the comments section of a survey.

While not designed to measure experience, CES and NPS loyalty surveys are good at signaling whether an employee is satisfied. However, neither can diagnose why someone is dissatisfied, so you'll try to intuit what happened during the transaction that made them unhappy. Nor can these "one-liners" show you how to improve delivery to satisfy someone.

But that isn't even their biggest problem. Relying solely on these "one-liners" can give you a false sense of security; worse, you could waste resources taking action on something that isn't a problem. (My prior "Dan the Technician" story.)

Why you should avoid CSAT (aka, Kano Model.)

In 1984, Kano produced a model for product satisfaction. Many well-meaning people unfamiliar with psychometrics try to create satisfaction surveys based on the Kano model. If you fall into this category, know you're not measuring IT satisfaction or QoE efficiently or effectively.

Kano-derived CSAT is a complex model developed for product management — its creator (Dr. Kano) says not to use it to measure service (IT) satisfaction! Most IT organizations using this approach are unaware of the totality of the model and are not getting true, actionable insights into their IT function.

I side with Dr. Kano and advise against using CSAT (Kano model derived) when measuring IT solution experience.

Your instruments are surveys — questionnaires used to measure satisfaction, including questions, response options, and guidance.

Your surveys must be reliable, valid, and unbiased to accurately capture the information needed for improvement. You probably shouldn't create your survey instruments on your own, or use variations of CSAT surveys derived from the Kano model, so let's focus on NPS and CES, the two heavyweights used in IT today.

NPS and CES, when applied correctly, are very useful in identifying perceptions of dissatisfaction. They're not diagnostic, however. That takes a complete psychometric instrument like SERVQUAL.

NPS and CES, the odd couple of IT satisfaction.

It's not a question of either or, but rather when and why. NPS takes a broader strategic IT view, while CES looks at the IT operational details of the employee experience. Both metrics provide valuable insights but for different reasons. NPS is more about IT strategic decision-making, and CES is more about operational IT recovery and improvement.

NPS is a strategic tool. Its focus on understanding loyalty and advocacy gives a high-level view of IT sentiment and brand perception.

Its high-level view helps NPS guide IT-level decisions — think about identifying areas for improvement, prioritizing initiatives, and understanding the overall health of the IT-business relationship. IT leaders should use NPS to assess long-term employee loyalty and drive strategic actions.

CES is for operational improvements. It measures digital employees' efforts to do tasks or solve IT issues. CES provides information about the operational efficiency of IT touchpoints or processes. It helps find pain points, streamline operations, and reduce digital friction.

Organizations should use CES to identify and address IT operational challenges, improve IT processes, and boost digital employee experience faster and more tangibly.

While they work well together, even if you use them correctly, they can still fail to guide the improvement of our digital employee experience in several ways:

- **Both arose from marketing consultants seeking to measure end-customer loyalty, not satisfaction.** While IT leaders use both for satisfaction today, they're primarily brand external-customer loyalty tools built for marketers.
- **They can be misleading because they measure transactional satisfaction, not the overall quality of experience.** You cannot trend success with a transaction and know employees are satisfied with the rest of your IT solution delivery chain!
- **They keep you from using better instruments.** They predict loyalty well enough to be helpful, as mentioned previously. That's enough for some people, but usually, IT providers need more, especially for today's digital employees and their complex digital workplace solutions.
- **NPS and CES measure different things.** While NPS and CES cross-reference into portions of RATER, they are not equivalent in predicting experience satisfaction. NPS seeks to measure purchase intent, while CES aims to measure effort. NPS is more commercially focused, while CES is more customer service oriented.

- **CES claims to be better at loyalty than NPS and suitable for support functions.** Its brand loyalty predictions are consistent across industries, regions, and languages. CES is similar to NPS, and research shows it indexes highly to two of the five RATER factors: Reliability and Responsiveness. That's why CES is often better at measuring IT support functions, for example. Still, not a great measure of QoE, but a decent indicator of IT satisfaction. I recommend CES to my clients.

- **NPS is an excellent measure of Assurance.** NPS indexes highly to Assurance (the "A" in RATER.) NPS is helpful, but it's not a full measure of QoE, as it only hits one of the five RATER determinants of satisfaction. NPS is most useful when used as designed: a buyer has direct freedom of choice — as in purchases. It's less effective in captive situations where the person surveyed doesn't have similar freedom of choice — for example, internal IT support situations. I don't recommend using NPS for IT solutions or digital employee experience.

- **They're commercial, owned by consulting companies.** Commercial products are great if you want to use consultants but less so if you want to build your team's capabilities.

- **They're remedial instead of diagnostic.** They capture the pulse of your employees after a service encounter or a transaction but offer few clues as to what's driving dissatisfaction or how to resolve it. They're not diagnostic because they can't show expected service levels or causes of experience satisfaction, dissatisfaction, or what you must do to fix things. All you know is if that transaction was acceptable or not, which, while necessary, is insufficient.

SERVQUAL shows how to think about experience satisfaction and how to measure it, manage it, diagnose it, and improve it.

SERVQUAL isn't a point-in-time satisfaction measure like NPS or CES. It's a diagnostic instrument to measure consumer attitudes (feelings) about their experience (multiple individual assessments of satisfaction and dissatisfaction.) Its maximum survey comprises 66 questions with a "100 points" distribution approach to understand RATER element values.

You can achieve many SERVQUAL benefits with its SERVPERF cousin (22 questions) or my QUIKQUAL (5 questions.) It's proven to be the basis for determining experience satisfaction for any service, including IT solutions.

The ZoT allows us to mimic disconfirmation, and its Gaps Model provides actionable targets for performance improvement; it can seem complicated to the uninitiated, but no more so than any other IT troubleshooting tool!

The three amigos of IT satisfaction.

You can measure your IT-business relationship, digital friction at the IT solution level, or diagnose the sources of IT dissatisfaction with either. You can also use all three as a complete solution to vexing IT experience problems — or for new solutions. Think of the three options as your IT satisfaction styles. The style you choose comes down to your goals:

1. **CES helps identify IT operational improvements.** It's great when you want to spot potential improvement opportunities in employee IT experience or optimize IT solutions, resolve issues, and streamline processes. It assesses user effort to pinpoint areas for improvement in IT. It also provides

insights into IT reliability and responsiveness. CES prioritizes problem resolution over strategy. Note that focusing on digital friction won't give you the whole picture for IT satisfaction.

2. **NPS measures trust and support from your business peers.** It's handy when focusing on your IT strategy and strengthening relationships between IT and the business. You can learn which customers are advocating for it. You can see your relationship's strength by looking at the trust level. This approach is more strategic than operational because it prioritizes loyalty over individual issues.

3. **SERVQUAL is a tool that helps design and diagnose digital employee experiences.** It gathers information about IT expectations and looks for signs of digital friction, low customer advocacy, or poor business-IT relationships. It looks at the IT experience employees require, expect, and perceive. It's the best way to measure digital employee experience. Other tools may have "one-line" surveys built in, but sorting out specific DEX problems and why they happen calls for more data collection and analysis.

Each tool serves a distinct purpose and has a different style of use when evaluating IT satisfaction. Yet they all have a role, as Figure 4-1 shows.

FIGURE 4-1. Using Transaction and Cumulative Satisfaction Tools to Resolve Digital Friction

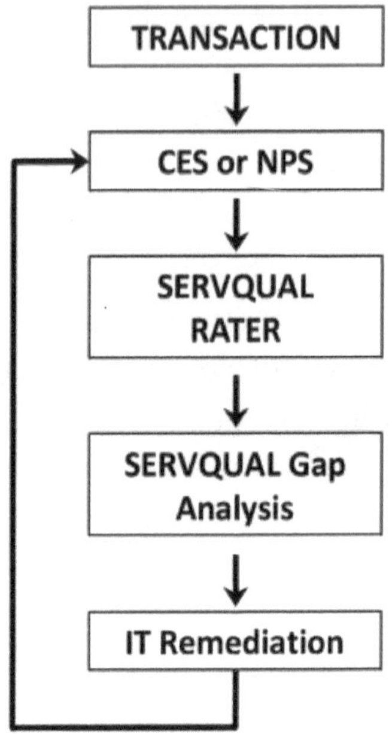

Here's a breakdown of each component in Figure 4-1:

1. **Transaction:** A specific interaction or exchange between a user or customer and IT, such as a support or feature request or any other engagement activity.
2. **CES or NPS:** CES is a metric used to measure a customer's effort to accomplish a task or resolve an issue. It helps evaluate the ease of working with an organization from the customer's perspective. NPS is a metric used to measure loyalty. Track these metrics over time to learn about satisfaction at customer and user levels.
3. **RATER:** An acronym for the five determinants of QoE that SERVQUAL manages. SERVQUAL is a popular framework used to assess consumer quality of experience.
4. **Gap Analysis:** A process that compares an organization's actual performance with its desired or expected performance.

When removing digital friction, gap analysis identifies discrepancies or gaps between user expectations and IT delivery efforts.

5. **IT Remediation:** Actions taken to address or resolve any issues identified during the gap analysis phase. In this context, IT remediation specifically focuses on using technology or service solutions to improve employee experience, streamline processes, or enhance the overall digital employee experience.

The following Satisfaction Story shows a real-world use case where multiple approaches solved a complex IT satisfaction problem.

***

Satisfaction Story: *From Digital Friction to Smooth Sailing*

Background: A shipping company's HR portal was causing digital friction for employees trying to find benefits information, resulting in unhappy employees and lost productivity. The company needed to identify the root cause of the digital friction and find a solution to improve the portal's effectiveness. They used a popup CES survey after IT transactions to assess employee experience and tracked satisfaction and complaints in a spreadsheet. If an employee had a poor experience, a follow-up survey using SERVQUAL examined the five RATER determinants of QoE. IT ran the survey as an interview or focus group to gather qualitative data. They used the Gaps Model to discover where the employee's voice got lost in the portal life cycle, including strategy, design, transition, and operation.

Results: Using CES to detect digital friction during portal transactions, such as planning paid time off and checking healthcare benefits, identified employees struggling with the portal. RATER evaluation led to employee complaints that the benefits portal was difficult to navigate (Tangibles), its pages loaded too slowly (Responsiveness), and results often contained outdated information (Assurance.) It also found that Reliability and Empathy were low, indicating that the portal didn't provide the same level or structure of information for all topics and that HR ignored employee feedback. The Gap analysis showed that the primary cause was a missing service concept from Gap 1, which led to unclear design specifications for workflows between teams.

Conclusion: Using CES, RATER, and the Gaps model, the company identified the root cause of the digital friction, took corrective action to improve the portal's usability and effectiveness, and made internal IT changes to ensure better communications and resource allocations. The solution involved learning what information structure employees needed to succeed and using a consistent information structure for that portal content. By leading with satisfaction, IT solved the portal's issues.

***

Your opinion of your solution's success is irrelevant unless your users tell you they're successful.

When you reach this point, the easy control points are up on the board, and people start tilting into more technical features or IT solution benefits. That's not what we're here for, however. In this step, we aim to understand user perception of the IT solution you're trying to improve. To do that, you need to know what you have control over and what you don't.

"When do you notice a pin least? When it's in a pincushion."

— *Hercule Poirot*

Most of the time, something will surprise you, something you had never thought about. And that's precisely the reason for this exercise. The best ideas about improving satisfaction will come from dissatisfied users, not engineers sitting in another building, state, or country.

Concentrate on perceptions of dissatisfaction rather than satisfaction.

Remediation presupposes IT dissatisfaction. Yet one critical mistake I've seen too many times is focusing on satisfied users. This is the wrong approach. Improving IT satisfaction means you need to focus on dissatisfaction. The causes of satisfaction are different from those causing dissatisfaction. Understanding these causes helps us improve IT. The causes of dissatisfaction are not necessarily the obverse of the reasons for satisfaction — and we need to know both!

For example, Reliability is more often a source of dissatisfaction than satisfaction. In other words, increasing it may not improve digital employee experience or IT satisfaction. But not having enough of it will cause significant dissatisfaction.

The relationship between satisfied and dissatisfied is why disconfirmation using RATER is so critical to your success at achieving and maintaining a great digital employee experience. It also means you can't treat satisfaction and dissatisfaction as opposites.

The opposite of satisfied with IT isn't dissatisfied; it's apathy, likewise for IT dissatisfaction. The reason is that IT solutions are the means to an end, not an end in themselves.

As we're so fond of saying within IT circles, our solutions are mere "tools." Few users will ever fall in love with their digital workplace kit. I can't imagine a person getting a thrill logging into a meeting. But I've seen and felt firsthand frustration with workplace solutions — as have you!

This matters to IT satisfaction and digital employee experience: the opposite of dissatisfaction is no dissatisfaction, and the opposite of satisfaction is no satisfaction. A rock-solid 2.5s page load time for a user who expects between 1 and 5 seconds isn't a source of satisfaction; it's the cause of no dissatisfaction. The tool does its job without creating digital friction. It fades into the background, and the user doesn't think about it. If you made it one second, users wouldn't be more satisfied. Nor would they be more dissatisfied — until it rises or impedes their expectations (aka what it takes to do their job.)

The balance point is what you must discover and maintain. For each RATER determinant, there is a "perfect" setting for your IT solution as consumed by a given workgroup doing the same job.

Balance IT solution fitness for use and purpose.

Fitness for Use (FFU) describes IT solutions that meet quality standards. *Fitness for Purpose* (FFP) describes solutions that meet consumers' needs and requirements. Together these concepts explain the levers to move to improve your IT delivery.

Fitness for Use ensures that an IT solution meets its specifications. Reliability and Tangibles are key metrics that measure how well the solution meets agreed-upon standards. FFP is about providing an IT solution that meets its consumers' needs and expectations. FFP primarily addresses Assurance, Empathy, and Responsiveness. These three RATER determinants measure how well IT understands and responds to user and customer needs and concerns. They're essential indicators.

Sometimes, there might be digital friction — for example, if the interface is complicated. That can impact user experience, which falls under the "Tangibles" determinant of the RATER model. But as long as users can still get their job done, even with some digital friction, you could be okay if you maintain consistent performance and keep delivery in the ZoT.

Of course, if the digital friction is so bad that it affects the solution's Reliability — if it's going down all the time or keeps throwing you errors, etc. — that's a different story. If "Fitness for Use" isn't there, you must re-engineer the solution to get the job done reliably and accurately.

Understanding digital employee experience is understanding the difference between perceptions and expectations across the five determinants. The good news is that if you humbly and respectfully engage your users, ask and listen to them, they will tell you precisely what you should do to thrive.

Addressing digital employee perceptions and dissatisfaction for enhanced IT Satisfaction.

You must remember the sequence shown in Figure 4-1.

Measuring IT satisfaction differs from measuring digital employee experience (QoE), which takes a series of activities related to assessing the experience of a user workgroup or IT solution. There is no single answer to IT satisfaction measurement, no "one number to track." It's essential to think of various possibilities that could result in better results.

Each solution must be adjusted to fit the unique needs of your organization. In this step, we looked at numerous ways to calculate and improve IT satisfaction. From surveys to worker feedback schemes, many techniques can help us understand the requirements and desires of our digital staff.

Our voyage is just beginning! The next step is to uncover what those experience expectations might be. In the next step, we will look into SERVQUAL more deeply and learn how it can give us the information we need to build a more satisfying IT experience for our digital staff.

STEP 5. UNCOVER EXPERIENCE EXPECTATIONS

IT satisfaction isn't a number; it's a collection of emotions. Pursuing a better digital employee experience takes what looks like an obstacle and turns it into a significant win.

What experience do employees believe you'll deliver?

That's a proactive question. It's future-looking and a question asked too seldomly. To understand the expectations of digital workplace employees, we can conduct surveys, interviews, and focus groups to gather feedback and insights on their needs and preferences. We can also analyze operational data on their interactions with IT solutions and use that information to inform improvements and updates.

But your success with IT satisfaction depends on changing your viewpoint. If you commit to the new perspective, you'll be more successful.

> "Embracing digital employee expectations unlocks success; ignoring them is a recipe for stagnation."
>
> — *Completely Satisfied*

In this step, we'll learn what positive and negative experiences look like and how to examine a digital workplace solution using RATER. The five RATER determinants reflect the overall perception of experience quality in digital employee use of IT solutions.

Unraveling the mystery of user satisfaction.

The first step is determining whether a digital employee (customer or user) is satisfied or dissatisfied, which is relatively easy using CES or NPS.

The second step, however, is more challenging as it involves understanding the reasons behind the boundaries users set. Luckily, an easy way to gain this knowledge is to ask them! Ask your users directly to understand better what they want from their IT experience. You can do this using questionnaires and interviews. You can't do it for everyone, nor can you do it too often.

But by gathering this feedback, you can make more informed decisions about allocating your resources and improving your IT capabilities to meet the needs of your consumers.

Digital employee experience got you down? Let's raise the bar with RATER!

Now is an excellent time to understand what the RATER framework represents to you, your teams, digital employees, end-customers, and your company.

Figure 5-1 reflects the experience profile for a collection of PC (Personal Computer) users. I use these for explanations, and I don't recommend you use them as-is. As an example, we'll use it from here on, but as mentioned before, every organization, workgroup, tool, and feature can have its RATER experience profile. You'll need to discover your allocation as required. More on doing that later on in Step 7.

FIGURE 5-1. Example RATER Experience Profile for PCs

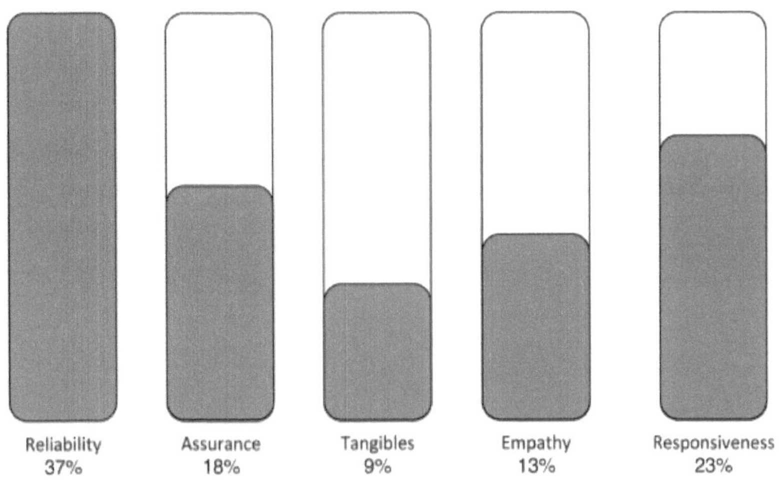

Figure 5-1 also illustrates some subtle points. We all know the importance of "user interface design" and "ease of use." We in IT often think that's what matters most to users and digital employee experience. But notice how low Tangibles are in importance compared to the other four factors. And I've mentioned how NPS aligns with Assurance (18% of QoE in Figure 5-1) while CES lines up with Reliability and Responsiveness (60% of QoE).

Outside of the obvious, what each of the five RATER determinants represents depends upon what we're examining. Like satisfaction, it's context-sensitive. If you want to improve your IT capabilities and meet the needs of your consumers, you need to understand what they want clearly. And to get that, you must ask them.

A questionnaire asking consumers about the five determinants can provide valuable feedback that helps you improve DEX. You can ask about perceptions and expectations at the same time, too, as we'll see later. But that's not all — analyzing the five RATER dimensions gives you even more insights.

RATER gives you a complete picture of user satisfaction and helps you make informed decisions about improving your IT capabilities. To enhance and align your IT resources with consumer needs, don't ignore the power of user feedback and the five RATER dimensions! They can make a big difference in delivering a satisfying user experience.

Let's see how with a case of a typical IT problem.

RATER in Action: A Case Study in Diagnosing IT Satisfaction

For the rest of this section, imagine your team has just released a new Business Intelligence (BI) system. You and your entire organization are very proud of getting this solution implemented and out to your business partners in record time.

But after a few days, employees start reporting significant frustrations and challenges with your shiny new BI masterpiece. They complain about the system's data accuracy, consistency, and performance.

You initiate a RATER evaluation focusing on its core functionality — tasks related to data retrieval, report generation, system responsiveness, and the ability to make better decisions. Your goal is to identify pain points and areas of high effort and dissatisfaction that indicate potential issues.

First up is Reliability.

The Reliability of your IT offerings is paramount.

Reliability means consistency and dependability, and IT's ability to perform its required functions under stated conditions for a specified period. Reliability is delivering the promised IT solution accurately and dependably. To employees, it means feeling confident they can do their job with what you provide them.

Reliability is often the most crucial determinant, accounting for approximately 37% of digital employee experience in our example RATER profile. Generally speaking, those activities directly impacting availability, capacity, security, and continuity will affect Reliability.

Continuing our BI implementation story, here's an example of how Reliability could appear to them.

***

Satisfaction Story: *Business Intelligence System Reliability Woes*

Negative User Experience: One aspect of Reliability that caused a negative user experience in the BI application was frequent data inconsistencies. Users often encountered discrepancies between report data and the source systems' figures. This inconsistency led to confusion and mistrust between teams, impacting their confidence in the system's Reliability. Users had to spend significant time manually cross-referencing data from multiple sources to ensure accuracy, resulting in delays in decision-making and decreased productivity.

Improvement and Positive Experience: The IT department took action to improve data reliability. They analyzed the data integration pipelines and found areas with possible errors. They added automated checks and validations at each data transformation and loading stage.

They also met with business stakeholders to establish data quality standards and conducted regular audits. As a result of these efforts, users experienced a decrease in data inconsistencies. They gained more confidence in the accuracy of the BI reports.

These changes enabled them to make faster decisions based on reliable data, leading to greater efficiency and better business outcomes.

***

Your digital employees are putting their jobs and family's futures on the line when they rely on IT. So, it's crucial to ensure the basic functionality of your IT solutions.

From an IT delivery quality perspective, examples of Reliability include providing service warranty and utility as promised:

- Ensuring availability of IT infrastructure as per XLAs and SLAs
- Delivering uninterrupted IT services, minimizing downtime
- Maintaining data integrity and security
- Conducting regular backups and implementing disaster recovery measures
- Proactively addressing performance issues and bottlenecks
- Implementing redundant systems and failover mechanisms for high availability
- Monitoring system health and performance metrics

As an IT leader, you want to ensure your IT solution is always available during the promised time. You must be transparent about any downtime and work to minimize it. And, of course, your IT solution should do whatever it does well.

As their IT provider, can you be relied upon to provide solutions your users are confident will be available and ready to use when needed? Example questions you can ask yourself to get insight into Reliability include:

- Does IT deliver on its promises?
- Are specifications given to customers and users correct?
- Are outputs, statements, reports, and performance free of error?
- Does IT perform the right the first time?
- Is the level of IT performance consistent across all staff members?

Assure digital employees that you're trustworthy.

Assurance is consumer confidence in the technology, support services, and solutions IT provides. Evidence of Assurance might include honesty about outages and service capabilities, the accuracy of support answers, etc. The assurance of IT expertise, commitment to security and privacy, and excellent support are crucial for a good digital experience.

It accounts for approximately 18% of the QoE in our example, and its importance to consumers increases proportionally as BVaR increases. (Remember to discover your unique values by workgroup and solution!)

To employees, it means having confidence in the IT technology and support services they use.

Building assurance should be a focus of IT leadership and teams when testing products, services, and solutions. It involves honesty about outages and capabilities and accurate answers to support inquiries.

***

Satisfaction Story: *BI Assurance Questions*

Negative User Experience: A critical aspect of Assurance that resulted in a negative user experience in the BI application was a lack of data integrity and security measures. People expressed worries about the vulnerability of sensitive business data. They had doubts about the accuracy and reliability of the information presented. This lack of Assurance weakened user confidence in the system's ability to protect and provide trustworthy data. People felt reluctant to rely on the BI application for critical decision-making and were hesitant to use it.

Improvement and Positive Experience: The IT department took many steps to ensure data security and trustworthiness. They provided limited access to sensitive data and set up authentication protocols and encryption mechanisms. IT did regular quality checks to ensure data was accurate and implemented data cleaning processes. IT trained users on proper data handling and informed them of the security features and protocols.

As a result, users gained confidence in the BI application. They believed IT built a trustworthy solution and felt they could now use BI data for important decisions. Their confidence created a positive digital employee experience that encouraged more people to use the BI application, speeding up business value.

***

Assurance examples include:

- Making consumers feel safe in their transactions
- Knowing how to answer consumer questions
- Building confidence in IT Leadership
- Developing highly skilled and knowledgeable IT teams
- Implementing robust security measures to protect user data
- Enhancing usability and user experience of IT interfaces and applications
- Demonstrating compliance with laws, regulations, and industry standards

Remember that Net Promoter Scores primarily measure Assurance. Trust is another word people use in this context, as is loyalty. Assurance is also an emotional component of Reliability. Poor Reliability will lead, in time, to poor Assurance. Generally, Assurance ranks third in importance behind Responsiveness and Reliability. Example self-survey questions include:

- What steps have you taken to make your digital employees trust your team?
- Does your staff respect customer and user property, privacy, and individual beliefs and opinions?
- Can your team use your technology quickly and skillfully?
- Do you communicate honestly, own mistakes, and ensure they don't reoccur?
- Are those who interact with IT consumers attentive and polite?
- Are responses accurate and consistent with other reliable sources?
- Can customers and users have confidence that the solution

you provide operates correctly?

Tangibles still matter in digital workplaces.

Tangibles are the physical and human interface aspects of an IT or digital workplace solution. All IT solutions rely upon some tangible physical components. For example, a cell phone must have a big enough screen to utilize e-mail effectively. This "packaging" around your service and how it's used is critical. Well-done tangibility makes employees feel they can learn the IT solution easily and quickly so they can focus on their job.

User interfaces, manuals, and hardware are critical to the overall IT experience. While they are often the lowest contributor to our sample IT digital experience at 9%, users won't like your solution if you make it hard for them to use! To invest in your IT solution's ease of use, focus on its usability and intuitiveness of the interface and information architecture. It's also essential to consider classic CX and UX design best practices that aid users in getting their work done.

As mentioned earlier, in many cases, Tangibles are the least impactful, yet IT overspends due to their prominent presence.

***

Satisfaction Story: *Making BI Tangible*

Negative User Experience: The Tangible aspects of the BI app made for a poor user experience. The design was messy, the navigation was inconsistent, and the visuals were outdated. These problems made it hard for people to get around the app and understand the data displays. It was hard to find what they needed and to customize the interface for their needs. The clunky design made it hard for average users to get things done, making them frustrated and less satisfied with the application.

Improvement and Positive Experience: The IT department worked hard to upgrade the Tangible aspect of the business intelligence application. They wanted to improve the user experience by redesigning the user interface. So, the IT department put in the effort to understand user preferences and their pain points. They conducted user research and gathered feedback.

Based on this, they revamped the user interface. It now has a clean, intuitive, and modern design. Plus, the navigation is easy to use. Streamlined workflows by job, and data visualization techniques, were significant improvements cited by now happy users.

IT added customization options allowing users to personalize the interface according to their preferences. Each user group now easily navigates, interprets data, and personalizes the application. The result is a positive user experience. User satisfaction and engagement with the application have increased.

***

Tangibles relate to user interfaces, physical facilities, equipment, appearance, accessibility, and IT communications and materials. Examples include:

- Ensuring that IT systems and equipment are modern, up-to-

date, and in good working condition
- Designing user interfaces that are stylish, intuitive, familiar, visually appealing, and user-friendly
- Establishing a well-designed and user-friendly self-service portal or knowledge base with clear instructions and guidelines
- Implementing accessible IT solutions that consider readability, color contrast, and assistive technologies

You don't have to make your digital workplace solution "magical" or even pleasant, but it should be easy enough to use that it doesn't cause digital friction productivity problems. Your users (and customers) will thank you.

Example IT self-assessments can include:

- Is the solution easy to understand and use immediately, or does it require extensive training?
- Does the solution meet expectations for "look and feel"?
- Are you relying on up-to-date trends in usability and design?
- Is your digital workspace as well planned as your digital workplace?
- Are facilities attractive?
- Are written materials easy to understand?
- Is your technology modern?

Show some Empathy, please!

We must engage consumers by co-creating, soliciting, and listening to what they have to tell us. Empathy is a big deal in IT. It's more than being nice and "service with a smile." It's about understanding your users and recognizing them as the valued contributors to your personal and professional success that they are.

Customers, users, and partners who feel understood and appreciated by IT tend to contribute invaluable improvement insights. Say hello to the RATER Empathy dimension, making up about 13% of example IT digital experience.

To show Empathy, you must prioritize your consumers in every way. It's not about being obsequious but learning from those who use and depend upon your IT solutions. And showing that you care by acting on what they tell you!

One way to think about our BI case study is that IT Empathy drove it. The response shown by IT to own and fix the problems reported by the user community is a case study of Empathy!

***

Satisfaction Story: *Getting Empathetic*

Negative User Experience: Users felt neglected. They didn't get the help they needed when they had questions or ran into issues. IT support staff didn't know how to support them or understand the problems. This lack of empathy impacted the users' ability to make the most of the application. It lowered their overall satisfaction and robbed IT of vital intelligence that could have improved the BI solution.

Improvement and Positive Experience: As soon as IT leadership discovered the BI solution's problems, they took charge and led to a better digital experience. The IT department set up a helpdesk team to quickly answer questions and assist users. They also developed a BI knowledge base and user instructions that were easily accessible, enabling users to solve everyday problems.

Additionally, the IT department organized training sessions and workshops to educate users on utilizing the BI application. The emphasis on empathy and user support made users feel supported and heard, giving IT invaluable insights to improve the solution. It empowered BI users to utilize the application correctly and got them improved access to support and training.

As a result, users became more skilled and confident in using the application. Surveys indicated that users experienced higher levels of satisfaction and productivity.

***

Empathy is giving caring, individualized attention to your consumers. It centers on access, communication, understanding, and knowing your customers and users. Examples include:

- Adopting a customer-centric approach, prioritizing user needs and concerns
- Training IT support staff in active listening and understanding user issues
- Providing personalized and empathetic interactions, acknowledging frustrations
- Creating a non-judgmental environment for users to express concerns
- Developing user-friendly communication channels for prompt responses

- Anticipating user needs and proactively offering guidance and resources
- Demonstrating patience when assisting users of varying IT proficiency

Evidence of empathy might include encouraging open honesty and feedback and capturing and acting on user input to drive new features, functionality, and services. Showing empathy can help digital employees feel heard and believe IT takes action on the topics they raise. By doing so, we can improve our delivery and create a more positive digital experience for all our stakeholders. Being empathetic leads to higher digital employee experience, satisfaction, and loyalty.

- Do you have multiple ways to gather user and customer feedback?
- Do you use that feedback to improve your IT support and delivery?
- Do you include those who use your products, services, and solutions in your planning, design, transition, and operational activities? Or do you "do IT to them"? Human Resource led engagement scores reflect this.
- Do you encourage open, honest feedback from your consumers? Do you capture and use this input to drive new features, functionality, and services?
- Do you formally recognize user contributions?
- Is it easy to reach the appropriate staff person?
- Does your staff avoid using technical jargon when speaking with consumers?
- Is the level and cost of service consistent with what your consumer requires?
- Do your support solutions accommodate consumers' schedules?

Be Responsive and treat digital employees like the vital contributors that they are.

Responsiveness is providing IT solutions and services that are timely. Competence, courtesy, credibility, and security are all part of being responsive. Being quick to respond shows you value your employees' time. Everyone likes it when their needs are taken care of quickly and easily.

That's why reacting to requests within promised time frames, having speedy lookups, and low latency displays are essential. It makes people feel productive. Responding quickly also means offering IT services and solutions with no delays.

Poor data transmission rates make customers feel the provider isn't doing their job. Not responding to emails or online queries as promised can also appear unresponsive.

You want your employees to feel cared for, and responding on time fast is an excellent way to do so.

***

Satisfaction Story: *BI Responsiveness*

Negative User Experience: The business intelligence application had poor responsiveness. Users complained of a poor experience. The system was slow, and data retrieval and report generation took too long. People had to wait so long when working on big datasets or making complex reports that the system timed out. Not getting information on time kept them from making the best decisions. The poor responsiveness of the application made it hard for users to be productive, wasted time, and made them unhappy.

Improvement and Positive Experience: The IT department improved the user experience. They studied the system infrastructure and found places where it was slow or inefficient. Then, they made hardware and software upgrades.

IT increased server capacity, network bandwidth, and traffic prioritization. They made data retrieval and processing algorithms faster. They added caching and data compression to speed up data access. All these QoS adjustments had a positive effect on responsiveness, digital employee experience, and IT satisfaction.

Users noticed less waiting time and quicker system responsiveness. Employees could get the data they needed to make decisions quickly. In the end, user satisfaction, productivity, and efficiency increased.

***

Examples of IT actions that can improve Responsiveness include:

- Ensuring sufficient storage, networking, and infrastructure capacity
- Monitoring system performance metrics for timely issue identification
- Implementing load balancing mechanisms for optimized resource utilization
- Employing caching and content delivery networks (CDNs) for improved response times
- Establishing and meeting prompt response times according to XLAs/SLAs
- Implementing automated systems or chatbots for immediate user assistance
- Implementing self-service options for quick issue resolution
- Proactively communicating anticipated service disruptions

Responsiveness is generally second in importance to Reliability. IT service managers should emphasize Responsiveness and Reliability if there are real quality issues or there are limited resources to improve quality.

You can boost responsiveness by having a solid presence on internal social media channels and actively engaging with employees to preempt problems — an IT early warning system! Don't forget to prioritize email responses, and even consider implementing chat features for those who prefer not speaking with someone.

The Customer Effort Score (CES) can also be useful for measuring Responsiveness, accounting for about 23% of our sample DEX profile. So, ensure your support is consistent, adequate, and appropriate to improve support and operational Responsiveness and keep your users and customers happy.

Example questions you can ask yourself include:

- How completely and quickly does your staff respond to requests from consumers?
- Are there latency issues users must get used to when using their IT solution?
- When there is a problem, does the organization respond quickly?
- Are IT staff willing to answer questions?
- Are specific times for service accomplishments given?
- Are consumer situations treated with care and seriousness?

RATER helps IT leaders deliver better IT experiences.

As an IT leader, you always look for ways to improve your IT services and provide a better user experience. That's where the RATER model can be helpful. By examining the Reliability, Assurance, Tangibles, Empathy, and Responsiveness of your IT services, you can gain valuable insights into what your users expect and how to meet their needs.

Using the RATER model can help you achieve the following outcomes:

1. **Improved User Satisfaction:** By understanding your users' expectations across the five RATER dimensions, you can change your IT services to improve their overall satisfaction, productivity, and engagement.
2. **Better Resource Allocation:** Analyzing user feedback on the RATER dimensions can help you identify areas where you can allocate or reallocate resources to meet user needs — often reducing costs and improving productivity.
3. **Enhanced IT Capabilities:** By addressing the RATER dimensions, you can make changes that improve your IT capabilities, align them with user expectations, and optimize price and performance.

IT satisfaction is a collection of emotions, not a number.

Using RATER means collecting user feedback and using it to make decisions about improving IT capabilities. Understanding IT satisfaction is crucial. Using five RATER dimensions is a great way to measure it.

When you meet expectations, it creates a better digital experience for users. RATER is an effective tool for measuring IT satisfaction because it objectively assesses it. The tool allows you to gain insight into customer satisfaction levels, enabling you to make informed decisions about best meeting the needs of digital employees.

Additionally, RATER enables you to track customer satisfaction over time, allowing you to identify trends and areas of improvement. Lastly, RATER allows you to compare your IT satisfaction results against industry benchmarks, enabling you to identify areas of strengths and weaknesses so you can focus your efforts on improving customer satisfaction.

In this step, you learned what to measure (and what you're measuring!) Let's explore how to measure. In the next step, we'll explore how you can target a practical digital employee experience.

STEP 6. ENTER THE ZONE OF TOLERANCE

At first, achieving an excellent digital experience may seem paradoxical. However, the pivotal moment occurs when you realize that striving for perfection can impede progress. Instead, success lies in accepting a reasonable level of quality.

Did you know that every IT solution you provide can have unique performance requirements?

What's your range of acceptable IT performance?

Businesses that sell IT services to external marketplaces should try to deliver more than adequate experiences. They should aim high and make efforts to delight buyers where they can.

When combined with swift service recovery, exceeding expectations can help gain customers and keep them loyal.

However, exceeding employee expectations in corporate IT is always more costly. The blind pursuit of higher internal IT satisfaction scores is wrong. Sometimes, you even need lower scores to satisfy digital employees completely.

It's important to remember that employee satisfaction is crucial for external customer satisfaction and business success. If you don't meet employees' expectations, end-customers will be unhappy, leading to lost revenue and customer churn.

To achieve digital employee expectations, IT leaders must deliver reliable products and services that meet their employees' needs and invest in feedback opportunities to identify areas for improvement. In this step, we focus on using the RATER framework determinants of satisfaction to sort out precisely what digital employees want and need — and it's seldom "more" of whatever you're already doing.

You must discover how digital employees feel about your delivery. The Zone of Tolerance approach keeps employees satisfied without overspending.

Figure 6-1 shows concepts from the SERVQUAL model, a popular framework for assessing QoE. A critical aspect of the SERVQUAL model is the "Zone of Tolerance" concept.

FIGURE 6-1. Relationship of User Experience Expectations

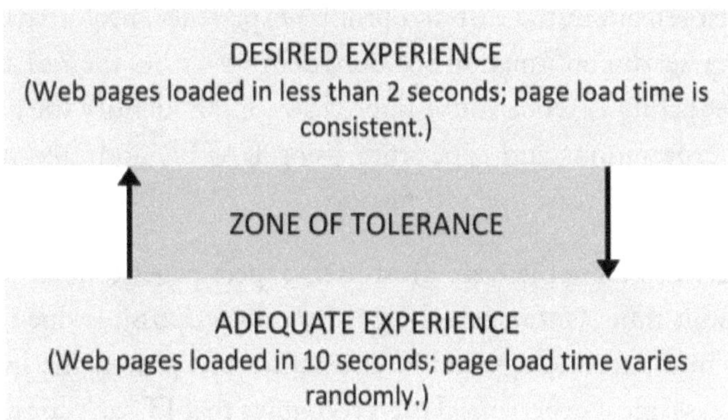

The space in the middle of Figure 6-1 is the Zone of Tolerance, the optimal range for IT delivery. The Zone of Tolerance refers to the degree of experience quality users consider acceptable between Desired and Adequate experiences. Desired is the experience users hope to receive. In contrast, Adequate experience is the minimum level of service quality that users find acceptable.

The difference between these two levels creates a tolerable delivery window within which users are willing to accept variations in experience quality.

Understanding the Zone of Tolerance is essential for IT leaders because it can help us identify and deliver against criteria — the range of quality users consider acceptable. You can meet user expectations and produce a satisfactory experience by measuring and managing quality within this zone. We complete the ZoT by adding the user's perception.

The digital employee's perception of how well we in IT are doing our job must remain in the ZoT to optimize experience, productivity, and profits. User disconfirmation positions delivery within the ZoT boundaries (hopefully!) Once you've done that, we can identify the gaps between expectations and experience using RATER and take steps to close them to increase user satisfaction.

Consider browsing the web. Most users expect pages to load without much wait time. Unfortunately, this isn't always possible due to limitations in the technology and infrastructure that powers the Internet. In this case, most experienced users recognize that IT can't consistently deliver the exact level of service they Desire. That's where the Adequate experience comes in — representing a lower threshold level still acceptable for most users.

Satisfied employees lead to loyal, satisfied end-customers (and vice versa!)

Feelings like "delighted," "very satisfied," "satisfied," "dissatisfied," and "very dissatisfied" depend on the employee's ability to do their job. Such attributes are a function of their expectations for Desired (upper) and Adequate (lower) experience boundaries, as shown in Figure 6-2.

FIGURE 6-2. Zones and Satisfaction Labels

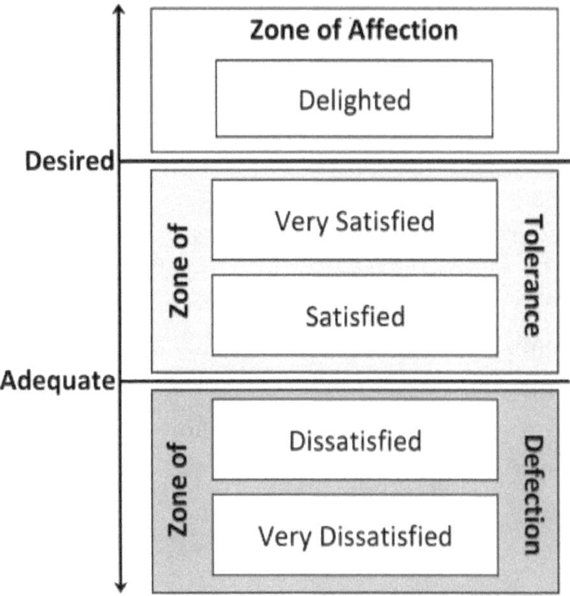

The three core zones in Figure 6-2 each represent a unique range of values. Every workgroup — often even when using the same IT solution — can have individual assessments for these ranges.

I've even seen examples of IT in brokerage organizations supporting very high-worth employees like stock traders with custom-tuned solutions per individual.

Here's what the three-zone ranges represent:

- **Affection** means you're probably over-delivering in an IT context. While it can please some employees, it might still be a potential problem from a cost perspective.
- **Tolerance** is usually, but as my preceding stock trader example shows, not always the ideal.
- **Defection** is plain bad, and you need to prioritize it. Employees in this zone usually disengage but haven't decided

to quit yet. If they're external customer contact personnel, their delivery typically follows their engagement and can lead to end-customer churn and lost profits.

In the zone: maximizing your digital workplace quality.

Let's start with the Zone of Tolerance. Discovering your ZoT is essential for maximizing digital workplace quality and finding the optimum experience for your digital employees. Users in this range are neither thrilled nor upset by your IT solution. Think of it as the "okay zone." For example, if you grab a sandwich at a deli and it's pretty good but not exceptional, you're probably within your tolerance zone for lunch on the run.

Your digital workplace's Zone of Tolerance, or ZoT, is where you want to deliver for optimum cost and performance. Anything below the Adequate border can prevent employees from doing their job correctly, stressing them out and hurting your business.

But going beyond the Desired boundary can mean wasting money and resources. If you deliver in the Zone of Affection, you could be over-spending or over-delivering and setting the wrong expectations.

Meanwhile, the Zone of Defection means that to users who feel this way, your solution is risking their job. Your solution prevents them from meeting the needs of end-users or end-customers. If this isn't corrected, these employees will quit. End-customers won't renew; worse, they'll start down-talking your company and take two, three, or five future clients with them. Performance in the Zone of Defection is all bad, and happily, that's what we're seeking!

The perils of adequate — when good enough is not enough.

Adequate experience refers to the minimum level of experience that a user expects to receive. This expectation comes from their past experiences and knowledge of what is acceptable in their context. Too close to Adequate may not please users, will probably cause digital friction, and can "hurt" to use — but work can get done. (As a side note, Adequate is helpful for disaster recovery and resilience planning.)

The primary problem with targeting the lower band of the ZoT is that there is little margin for error and recovery. You can wind up making yourself more work and displeasing users instead.

For example, if users are familiar with a collaboration tool that has always worked without significant issues, they expect it to continue functioning at that same level. But here's something to watch out for — if you deliver a higher experience, you just raised your bar and reset their expectations!

Consider a digital employee who uses a Customer Relationship Management (CRM) system to manage external end-customer data and interactions. An Adequate IT experience for this user would mean:

- Occasional system performance issues, such as slowdowns or minor glitches.
- Limited customization options or missing features that could enhance efficiency.
- Some difficulty when navigating through the CRM system interface.
- Annoyance and frustration due to the system's limitations.
- Ability to complete job responsibilities but with less-than-optimal ease.
- Feeling that the system falls short of expectations in terms of user-friendliness and reliability.

- Borderline dissatisfaction with IT.

***

Satisfaction Story: *Adequate Experience*

One user explains, "The system is usable most of the time, but it's got some issues. This may seem small, but it's a real pain. System-generated emails need formatting adjustments every single time — even when the content is correct. It only takes me like 10-20 seconds to reapply fonts and line spacing. But it adds up. I send 50 to 100 emails to clients every day! Why can't IT just fix it and do it right?"

***

In the above example, an adequate IT experience with the CRM system means employees can perform their job functions but must deal with digital friction.

But, if digital employees can't get Adequate IT experience, it can negatively affect both the employee and the organization. For example:

- **Reduced productivity:** Technical issues, slow system response times, or other IT-related problems can slow down or interrupt an employee's work, leading to wasted time and reduced productivity.
- **Frustration and stress:** Dealing with IT issues or struggling with poorly designed digital tools can cause users to feel frustrated, stressed, or demotivated.
- **Increased turnover:** If the IT experience is consistently inadequate, users may become dissatisfied with their job and decide to leave the organization, leading to higher turnover rates and associated lost revenue.
- **Poor end-customer experiences:** If digital employees

struggle to use IT systems or tools, it can negatively impact the quality of their interactions with your marketplace, clients, and business partners.

- **Reputation damage:** Repeated poor IT system and tool performance can also harm how your marketplace views your company, potentially leading to negative reviews, reduced loyalty, or difficulty attracting talent.

Great expectations: the minimum bar for experience quality.

Expected experience is what a user believes you will provide. Employees base their expectations on past experiences, word-of-mouth, and what you and your IT team tell them. For example, if a person has used a given solution before and it has always worked well, they will likely expect it to continue to work well. On the other hand, if they have recently heard negative feedback from others about it, they may lower their expectations accordingly.

IT leaders must understand and manage these expectations to ensure they provide a high-quality experience that meets expectations.

Keep your IT delivery in the Zone!

We establish the Zone of Tolerance by asking users specific questions about their upper and lower satisfaction levels across the five RATER determinants.

It's usually never a good idea to ask your consumers what they expect directly! It's much better to ask about "what good looks like" from their point of view. For example, we wouldn't ask, "What's your desired service level for the CRM system?" Nor would we ask, "On a scale of 1 to 5, what is your desired CRM performance?" Hopefully, the reason you shouldn't is obvious, but in case, people would usually say 5!

Instead, we'd ask very different (psychometrically valid) questions, using structures like this one, for example, "Excellent college computing technology teams will maintain fully-functional equipment and software," and ask the consumer to agree or disagree using a Likert scale. In this way, we build up the desired and adequate boundaries.

> "The perfect is the enemy of the good."
>
> *— Voltaire*

The outcome of such a survey or interview is a representation of acceptable IT performance ranges for each of the RATER factors. Our goal is to keep IT delivery within the upper and lower boundaries. You'll typically measure the ZoT by asking users how strongly they agree or disagree with questions about RATER components.

***

Satisfaction Story: *Designing for Experience*

Background: Earlier in my career, I worked around IBM programmable communications controllers in mainframe environments. I learned about expectation management from some of the best satisfaction technicians in the world — these people knew how to design and deliver a consistent experience.

Here's an example of how they did it. We were rolling out a new nationwide banking application. I didn't understand at first why they had us program delays into the system. Before going live, the system had blistering sub-second response times during testing, but IBM engineers had us tweak the code with built-in delays to make it always take just about 2.5 seconds.

Results: As we added more users, I began to understand why. We slowly backed out the 2.5 seconds to 1.5s, 1s, and none. Everybody had a consistent experience from the first user to the 10,000th. Everybody's perception was a consistent experience no matter when they gained access, where they worked or visited.

Conclusion: This system was rock-solid. It didn't flinch from the first user to the last user, and that's where I learned expectation management. That should be your goal too. Design an experience by determining in advance what performance will be. Then keep it that way.

***

Why over-delivering for IT users is usually the wrong approach.

I've found that many IT leaders believe that over-delivering and delighting IT users should be the ultimate goal. It's vital to challenge this notion and recognize that over-delivering isn't always necessary, cost-effective, or valuable for internal IT solutions.

While the intention may be to exceed expectations and delight IT users, the pitfalls of over-delivering include the following:

- **Unnecessary costs:** Over-delivering for IT users often incurs substantial additional costs. Investing in cutting-edge technologies, customizations, and extra features that exceed basic requirements can strain budgets and drain resources.

These costs don't always translate into a proportional increase in user satisfaction, productivity, retention, or profits. Sometimes you spend more and reduce IT satisfaction.

- **Complexity and support challenges:** Introducing an abundance of features and customization options can lead to increased complexity within the IT infrastructure. This complexity poses challenges for IT support teams, who must handle a variety of configurations, troubleshoot issues, and provide adequate training. The time and resources required to support these intricate systems operating at very high-performance levels can outweigh any potential benefits.
- **Challenges with overwhelmed users:** While the intention may be to delight IT users, over-delivering can sometimes have the opposite effect. An excessive number of features and customizations can overwhelm users, making it difficult for them to navigate and fully utilize the technology. Too much is as bad as too little. Busy interfaces can lead to frustration, reduced productivity, and a steep learning curve for new employees. Ultimately, it may hinder user adoption and satisfaction.

The pitfalls of not living up to expectations.

While over-delivering can have detrimental effects, it's essential to acknowledge that under-delivering isn't without its pitfalls. In pursuing cost-effectiveness, some organizations often inadvertently adopt an under-delivery approach when meeting IT users' technology needs. That can be as bad as over-delivering because under-delivering and being overly frugal can adversely affect business operations and overall success.

Under-delivering may seem like a short-term cost-saving strategy, but it often costs more regarding external customer loyalty and profits in the long run. Plus, outdated systems require frequent maintenance, face security vulnerabilities, and hinder scalability.

These factors can lead to increased downtime, higher IT support costs, and missed business opportunities — a vicious downward spiral. It's no coincidence that many failing firms have high technical debt and misfiring IT business solutions.

The pitfalls of under-delivering for IT users include:

- **Inadequate technology infrastructure:** By under-delivering and cutting corners, organizations risk providing insufficient technology infrastructure for their IT users. Outdated systems, limited functionality, and subpar performance can hinder productivity, collaboration, and the overall efficiency of digital workflows. This "technical debt" can lead to frustration among IT users and negatively impact the organization's bottom line.
- **Reduced user satisfaction:** When organizations prioritize cost-cutting over meeting the needs of IT users, IT satisfaction inevitably suffers. IT users may feel unsupported, hindered by outdated technology, and unable to perform their tasks effectively. Employees experience decreased motivation and engagement, increasing turnover and marketplace customer churn. Ultimately, the cost of low user satisfaction can far outweigh the savings gained from under-delivering.
- **Missed opportunities for innovation:** Under-delivering can mean missing out on opportunities for innovation and growth. By focusing on cost reduction, organizations may fail to leverage emerging technologies or invest in necessary

upgrades that could drive competitive advantage. A lack of investment in technology can stifle creativity, limit adaptability to changing market trends, and hinder the organization's ability to stay ahead of the curve.

Why meeting, not exceeding, employee expectations is your goal.

Digital workplaces are digital, but humans are analog. That's the difficulty with the IT satisfaction approaches used today. Why? Satisfaction is an emotional evaluation of how an IT solution matches someone's ideas about their expected experience.

> "Because customers and users define and decide IT quality and value, such determinations are relative, not absolute."
>
> — *Adapted from Heskett, J. L., Sasser, W. E., Schlesinger, L. A.*

Looking at metrics like "speeds and feeds" doesn't provide helpful info about how humans think. Worse, increasing a single number like CES or NPS inside an IT environment can increase costs without improving digital employee experience or productivity because you're not targeting the root cause of the low transaction scores.

The surprising benefits of sticking to what employees are willing to tolerate.

Employees will never gush over how fantastic your IT solution is and take a selfie standing next to it! The best you can hope is that they forget about it and focus on their job instead.

We aim to be reliable utilities like water and electricity — there when you need us. Remember, unless your electricity was out for the last six days when you flipped the light switch this morning, did the fact that the room lit up fill you with awe and joy?

Or did you not even notice it as you got going? That's our goal in IT, too.

- **Finding your balance point:** Overall, finding your sweet spot and sticking to what users are willing to tolerate can benefit businesses, from increased engagement to loyalty and end-customer referrals to greater efficiency and profitability.
- **Increased end-customer loyalty:** Businesses can build a loyal employee base that trusts and values their employer by consistently meeting user expectations within their Zone of Tolerance. Loyal employee satisfaction carries over into your marketplace.
- **More efficient use of resources:** By improving the quality of experience within the acceptable range of the Zone of Tolerance, you can avoid wasting resources on providing service levels that users may not value or appreciate, or worse, creating digital friction lowering IT satisfaction.
- **Lower retention costs:** By satisfying existing users and building engagement, you can reduce employee turnover and the costs of attracting new employees.
- **Improved word-of-mouth referrals:** Satisfied users are more likely to please or delight end-customers who will recommend your company to others, which can help to generate positive word-of-mouth referrals and bring in new end-customers. Note that the opposite is also true here!
- **Greater profitability:** You can provide cost-competitive solutions by meeting user needs and expectations within the acceptable range of the Zone of Tolerance.

The hidden costs of failing to keep delivery in the Zone of Tolerance.

I always say, "Good enough is perfect for most IT organizations." Settling for ZoT delivery leads to success. Striving to exceed user expectations and push into the Zone of Affection, or falling into the Zone of Defection, can be expensive mistakes. I advise keeping it in the ZoT for optimal user satisfaction and costs.

*****

Satisfaction Story: *Using the Zone of Tolerance to Improve IT Services and Control Costs*

Background: A mid-sized financial institution addressed declining employee satisfaction with IT services using the Zone of Tolerance approach. Here's how they improved service delivery.

1. **Established expectations:** Surveys and focus groups helped understand employee expectations for response times, system availability, functionality, and ease of use.
2. **Measured service quality:** RATER results assessed actual service quality compared to expectations.
3. **Defined the Zone of Tolerance:** Employee feedback defined the acceptable range of service quality.
4. **Identified service gaps:** They identified areas where delivery fell outside the acceptable range using the tolerance zone as a reference.
5. **Prioritized improvements:** Enhancement prioritization became a function of impact on employee satisfaction.
6. **Monitored:** Ongoing surveys and feedback mechanisms checked employee satisfaction and identified areas for further

improvement.

Results: By consistently delivering services within the acceptable range of the Zone of Tolerance, the IT department improved employee satisfaction without additional costs or new technologies.

Conclusion: This approach set realistic expectations, built trust, and met employees' needs effectively.

***

Taking action to center digital employee experience within the Zone of Tolerance.

The Zone of Tolerance (ZoT) concept is critical in achieving optimal digital employee experience.

- To begin, assess the current state of your organization's digital employee experience. Measure and gather feedback to identify the gaps between Desired and Adequate experience levels for each RATER factor. Your assessment provides a clear picture of your organization's ZoT boundaries and helps set realistic expectations. Use this data to refine XLA/SLA commitments.
- Next, focus on meeting the expectations of your employees within the ZoT. Strive to deliver consistent, reliable digital experiences within this acceptable range. Instead of chasing perfection, prioritize minimizing digital friction and providing a user-friendly environment that employees find satisfactory.
- Regularly communicate the importance of the ZoT and its impact on employee satisfaction and organizational success. Educate stakeholders on the significance of managing expectations within this zone. Raising awareness can give you

the support and resources to prioritize digital employee experience.

By taking these actions, you can create satisfying digital workplaces where employees thrive and productivity soars.

Remember, the ZoT framework provides a roadmap for success. Embrace it, adapt it to your organization's unique needs, and transform your digital employee experience within the acceptable boundaries of the Zone of Tolerance.

Figure 6-3 shows user perception of Reliability and Tangibles plotted against their ZoTs.

FIGURE 6-3. Different Zones for Dimensions

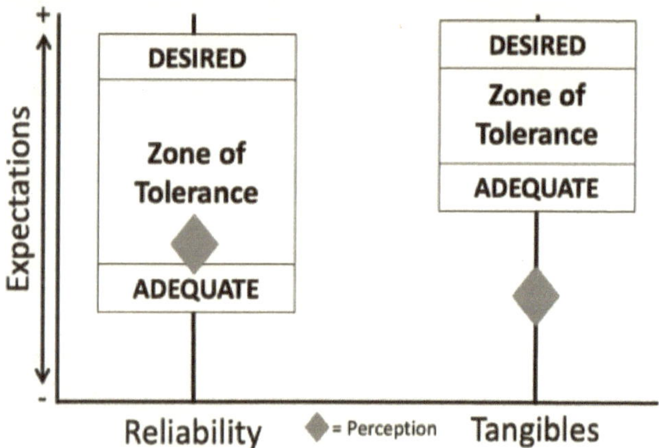

Notice the ranges in Figure 6-3. You can see your digital employee experience, which factor is causing low IT satisfaction, and what steps you need to take to resolve the issue. For clarity, I only show two of the five RATER determinants in Figure 6-3.

With dedication, collaboration, and continuous improvement, you'll elevate your organization's digital employee experience to new heights, driving success and satisfaction across the board.

This step taught us how the Zone of Tolerance concept is essential to attaining an optimal digital employee experience. Now it's time to take action and implement the insights gained. Let's move to the next chapter and apply the ZoT framework to your digital employee experience. It's time to dig into disconfirmation!

STEP 7. CONFIRM PERCEPTION MEETS EXPERIENCE EXPECTATIONS

You and your satisfaction team are approaching a crucial stage where many initiatives falter due to resistance from IT staff.

What quality of experience do you provide digital employees? After you've sorted out Desired and Adequate performance for an IT solution, the next step is to determine where perception falls. You do this by examining how users perceive and expect the five RATER dimensions we discussed earlier.

To measure these dimensions, you can use a survey that's pretty straightforward to complete. In this step, we'll learn how to analyze satisfaction to define and place our performance within the Zone of Tolerance.

Confirmation and Disconfirmation are new concepts for most.

As we saw earlier, disconfirmation refers to the perception of a gap between expectations and reality, whether a user's or customer's experience exceeds or falls short of their expectations.

The idea is that consumers have expectations, predictions, and perceptions about the QoE your IT solution will deliver. The question is, do those subjective personal assessments fall within the consumer's ZoT? And if not, why not?

You should expect push-back from the broader IT team now. It's the natural response when they feel called out or don't fully understand a new approach that might reflect poorly (at least initially) on their work. Engaging with your teams and showcasing positive results is essential to overcome passive resistance and build collaboration.

> "The most difficult thing is the decision to act; the rest is merely tenacity. The fears are paper tigers. You can do anything you decide to do."
>
> — *Amelia Earhart*

Confirmation is when our perceived (actual) experience comes close to our expected experience. Disconfirmation is when our perceived and expected experiences don't match up. It explains the relationship between your users' expectations for the solutions you provide and their perception of how well you're meeting those expectations.

Disconfirmation can happen in both positive and negative directions. If employees expect a certain level of performance, functionality, or user experience from an IT solution, and the experience exceeds their expectations, that would be positive disconfirmation. On the other hand, if the experience falls below their expectations, it would be negative disconfirmation.

In IT services, disconfirmation refers to keeping IT delivery within the Zone of Tolerance. To optimize experience and productivity, we must meet expectations, but to be cost-effective, we must stay within the ZoT. Beating expectations is usually counter-productive and confuses many who don't understand the RATER framework.

To effectively manage satisfaction with IT services, you must understand user expectations and monitor their experiences. By measuring the level of disconfirmation, IT service providers can identify areas where improvements are needed to meet expectations better and enhance their overall satisfaction with the solutions provided.

Putting the "service" in digital solutions improves satisfaction by meeting expectations.

When we talk about experience quality, there are a few other points to consider. We discussed "desired" and "adequate" experience expectations. But digital employees have another expectation regarding using an IT-provided digital workplace, their prediction of what they believe they will (or should) experience.

Predicted experience is the user's initial assumption or expectation of their experience. Prior experiences, knowledge of industry best practices, perceived benefits of using digital tools, and most importantly, what you and your team have promised, said, and advertised all shape user expectations for their experience. You have much more control over these expectations than you might think! Being honest and listening to users (aka Empathy!) goes a long way toward shaping what they expect from their IT solutions.

Figure 7-1 shows the relationship between Desired, Adequate, and Predicted experiences in disconfirmation. Each comprises all five RATER factors — one set for Desired, one for Predicted, and one for Adequate.

FIGURE 7-1. Confirmation and Disconfirmation

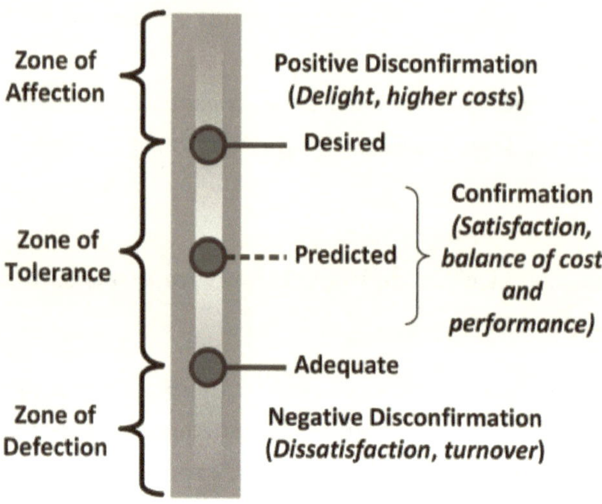

Figure 7-1 illustrates how users are unsatisfied with the service they're receiving if the gap between expectations and experience is negative. On the other hand, if the gap is positive, that means users are generally happy with the service they're getting.

- **Positive Disconfirmation** occurs when user perception of IT solution performance exceeds their expectation. For example, if an employee expects (predicts) a response time of one hour for an IT service request but receives a response within 30 minutes, they will experience positive disconfirmation. This positive experience can lead to higher levels of satisfaction and loyalty. However, suppose you drive performance above their desired level. In that case, employees will now expect that level of performance, and knowing that you can deliver it makes them dissatisfied when you don't, so be careful.
- **Negative Disconfirmation** occurs when the actual performance of the IT solution doesn't meet expectations.

For example, if a user expects a response time of one hour but has to wait for two hours, they will experience negative disconfirmation. This negative experience can lead to dissatisfaction and reduced levels of engagement.

But when there are significant discrepancies between what users expect and what they're experiencing, that's an opportunity to make improvements within the IT organization.

By addressing these gaps and working to meet user expectations more closely, you can enhance the quality of your IT services and better meet the needs of your employees.

Your user's perception is your reality, and you can shape it!

Perceived experience refers to a person's actual use of an IT solution compared to their expectations. It's the user's unconscious evaluation of the solutions Fitness for Use (FFU) and Fitness for Purpose (FFP) across the five RATER determinants.

It's the level of satisfaction documented by disconfirmation across the ZoT. If the experience meets or exceeds their expectations, they'll perceive it as good or excellent (positive disconfirmation.)

But they'll perceive it as poor or unacceptable if it falls short (negative disconfirmation.)

> "The customer's perception is your reality."
>
> — *Kate Zabriskie*

On the other hand, if their experience approximates their expectations, they'll perceive the IT solution as okay.

Figure 7-1 shows that uncovering user satisfaction assesses the gap between expectations for and of experiences. These concepts are vital for you and your "Satisfaction Team" to understand because this is how you measure experience quality and design digital solutions that meet or exceed employee expectations.

Like predicted expectations, several factors can influence a person's perceived experience because their needs can change. The term for these factors is "intensifiers." For example, if the books are closing and an accounting user has to get a particular report out on time to avoid penalties, their sensitivity to the ZoT can increase.

You must know about these "patterns of business activity" and consider them as you build and deliver your IT solutions.

Mind the gap: closing the chasm between expected and perceived experience.

QoE is the difference between consumer perception and expectation. If perception falls short of expectations, it signals potential internal and external dissatisfaction that could negatively impact productivity, retention, loyalty, and repeat business.

The gap between expected and perceived experience is "Gap 5", the Service or Quality Gap. Pay close attention to Gap 5 — by understanding and meeting user and customer expectations and continuously improving our delivery processes to match ZoT disconfirmation — more on Gaps and closing them in Step 9.

Balancing satisfaction and cost.

Understanding disconfirmation can help you balance satisfaction and costs. It's crucial because desired experience is often higher than the predicted experience for an IT solution.

It bears repeating that trying to delight users typically increases costs without increasing their performance. There is seldom an ROI to increasing satisfaction to desired or higher.

You can keep your customers and users happy and loyal by setting clear expectations, monitoring satisfaction, communicating proactively, and keeping your solutions in the zone.

Here are a few ways you can use this knowledge at your place of work:

- **Set clear expectations:** Ensure your customers and users understand what they can expect from your solutions. Define and share response times, availability, and the level of support they can expect. When digital employees have clear expectations, meeting them and avoiding negative disconfirmation is easier. Avoid embellishment; it's better to under-promise. Be honest, even if you know you need to do better.
- **Monitor satisfaction:** Track how happy customers and users are with your solutions. Use CES/NPS and other surveys, feedback forms, or check-ins. When you know how they feel about your IT delivery, you can improve to meet their expectations and avoid negative disconfirmation.
- **Communicate proactively:** When there are issues or delays, immediately communicate with customers and users. Let them know what's happening and when to expect a resolution to manage their expectations and avoid negative disconfirmation.
- **Continuously align and improve:** Review and analyze feedback to identify areas where you can improve the

experience outside the ZoT.

With RATER-based perception and expectations, you and your team can know what digital employees genuinely want and need; and see what needs to change.

Initially, it can be tough for IT folks to accept that "more" isn't how you deliver productive IT solution experiences.

But once you know what users expect from your solutions, you can start working to meet those expectations.

However, there's a point where meeting those expectations doesn't add any additional value for users. At that point, you've hit the threshold level of performance, and any further improvements are likely not worth the resources.

Much like gardening, it takes pruning to make IT satisfaction flourish.

The framework we've been using for surveys is SERVQUAL. It's a 22-question survey instrument to gather three data points per question across the five RATER determinants about users' adequate, desired, and perceived experience.

Typically, you measure Adequate and Desired annually and Perceived quarterly or bi-annually. By looking at such survey results, you can better understand how well your IT organization meets user needs and expectations.

Figure 7-2 is an example of one possible output aggregating all the users for a given workgroup. Note the RATER determinants in relationship to the lower (Adequate) and upper (Desired) boundaries shown as dotted lines. The ZoT is the space between dotted lines, and the heavy solid line represents the cumulative perceptions of a team of developers using an IT solution (IT workers are users too!)

FIGURE 7-2. Example RATER Experience Profile Plotted on ZoT

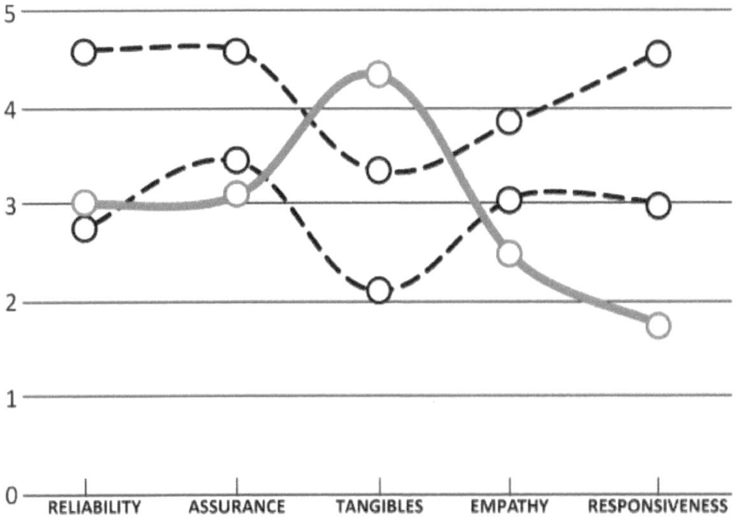

At a glance, Figure 7-2 provides critical management information for an IT solution's experience. The team behind this solution is most likely missing what matters to its users:

- The ZoT is tight for this workgroup.
- Reliability is barely adequate, and there's very little room for error on your part.
- Assurance, Empathy, and Responsiveness are low and probably negatively impact employee productivity — with all

the undesired knock-on implications for the rest of the business.

- Responsiveness is the most critical item to address right now.
- Tangibles are outside the ZoT, exceeding desired expectations. While you might delight employees with the solution's interface, the rest of the picture shows a different story for their entire experience!

Take a moment and reflect on Figure 7-2 and the preceding commentary.

Now, notice how you can diagnose digital employee experience like a radiologist examining an x-ray! This is an unhappy workgroup, frustrated and not as productive as they could be. Notice also that you can see where and why you need to take action — the ZoT makes it simple to spot where you need to focus your team on improving.

But also, as shown in Figure 7-1, working with diagnostic data can make some teams feel "targeted" or called out. For example, the UI team for the IT solution above likely thinks they're doing great. They're overdelivering for sure, and they may be overspending too!

Consider also that core functionality is borderline lacking, and IT isn't responsive — digital friction could be high.

Lastly, Empathy being significantly outside the ZoT means you and your team aren't listening to what this workgroup wants to tell you!

The single best metric you've never heard of is Digital Effort Score.

Digital Effort Score (DES) is an actionable satisfaction metric I designed specifically for IT Leaders. Imagine taking Figure 7-2 and turning it into a number. That's what you get with DES. It reflects digital employee effort or waste due to unoptimized IT solutions and workflows (digital friction.) Figure 7-3 shows how DES logically consolidates RATER scores — in this example from Figure 7-2 — considering each factor's weighting, ZoT, and perception.

FIGURE 7-3. Digital Effort Score

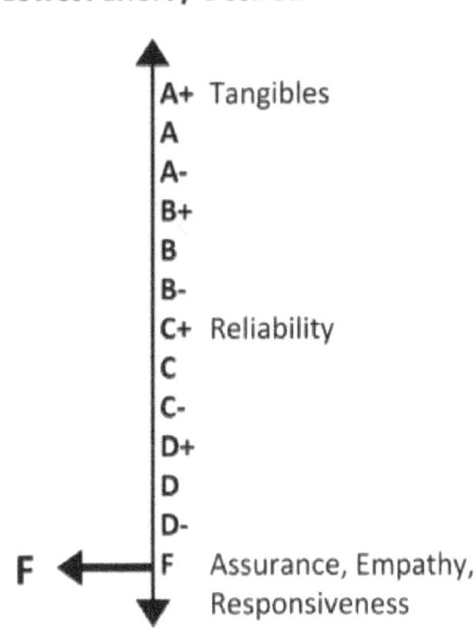

The ranking in Figure 7-3 comes from the example RATER experience profile shown in Figure 7-2. Can you figure it out? (Hint, the scale in Figure 7-3 is in order of ease of use, which means highest to lowest scoring. Then the importance weighting for each factor results in the DES score, calibrated to Desired and Adequate ratings overall. The high scores aren't enough to recover from the low scores and pull the entire solution down.)

You can get a free spreadsheet at hankmarquis.com that shows how to create your IT solution DES score based on the RATER profiles you develop. DES adapts to workgroups, is diagnostic (unlike CES or NPS), and psychometrically valid. DES reflects the time and energy spent making a digital workplace solution work—from both provider and consumer perspectives.

A lower DES on the consumer side aligns with a higher value on the provider side. And vice versa.

I coined the term DES a while back because there are multiple DEX definitions, and most are open to interpretation. Plus, the cause of DEX, digital friction, confuses many. I like DES because it visualizes co-creation and value on a prosumer scale. I also like that it makes IT satisfaction scores more relatable and actionable.

IT leaders can have one metric that reflects employee success, engagement, productivity, customer loyalty, and business value.

In contrast, consider how we measure, track, and deliver DEX and IT efforts today with SLA, XLAs, and various technical and operational tools, with an appended collection of IT satisfaction and employee engagement surveys. We already know how our employees and end-customers measure DES — they vote with their feet!

Your keys to DEX success.

Figures 7-1, 7-2, and 7-3 are the three keys to your success. Taken together, you have almost all that you need to lead with IT satisfaction:

1. **DEX has a simple QoE = P - E formula.** Why does having a formula matter? Because a formula makes complex tasks more straightforward. It helps us visualize leading with satisfaction. It organizes work neatly by focusing on essential parts, following a predictable method, working more efficiently, solving problems effectively, and helping us learn — and lead — better.

2. **RATER determinant expectations are diagnostic.** A diagnostic approach helps us understand complex problems by carefully examining and analyzing them, identifying key factors, finding patterns or clues, making informed evaluations, and using this knowledge to find practical solutions.

3. **DES is actionable.** An actionable approach empowers us to take practical steps toward solving complex problems. It involves identifying specific actions we can take, setting clear goals, creating a plan, implementing it with determination, and continuously adapting and refining our efforts based on feedback and results.

Managing digital employee experience = proactively ensuring perception meets expectations.

In the "three keys to success" in the preceding step, I mentioned you have almost all the ingredients to lead with IT satisfaction. The final component is your satisfaction team. You and your IT satisfaction team need to reach out to the broader IT team and stakeholders to create awareness about the new approach and its benefits. Educate them on confirming the importance of diagnostic QoE in delivering completely satisfying IT solutions.

Here's a roadmap. The order depends on your unique situation and where you and your teams are right now, but make sure you tick the box on these milestones:

- **Communicate the objectives and goals** of the new approach clearly, emphasizing how it benefits both users and the IT team. Keep everyone informed about the progress and successes achieved through regular updates and transparent communication channels.
- **Foster a collaborative environment** where IT staff can openly discuss their concerns and provide input. Encourage them to share their experiences and ideas for improvement.
- **Establish clear expectations** and communicate them to users and the IT team using RATER factors to explain satisfaction goals and how users will experience them. Clarity helps avoid misunderstandings and negative disconfirmation.
- **Provide the IT team with the necessary resources, training, and support** to help them embrace the new approach. Empower them to take ownership of user satisfaction and provide them with the tools and knowledge to deliver exceptional experiences.
- **Regularly measure IT satisfaction** and feedback using surveys, feedback forms, and direct interactions. Analyze the results to identify areas for improvement and take action accordingly.

- **Encourage a culture of continuous improvement** by actively seeking feedback, identifying gaps, and implementing necessary changes. Consistently review and align IT services with user expectations to ensure ongoing satisfaction. DES is invaluable here.
- **Acknowledge and celebrate achievements and positive outcomes** from the new approach. Highlight instances of improvement. Ensure it was cost-effective and appropriate, and when so, showcase the value delivered by the IT team.

Unleashing business potential through optimal digital employee experiences.

Remember that you can create a positive and satisfying digital employee experience by actively engaging and involving the broader IT team, aligning services with user expectations, and using what you learn to improve your delivery.

We've examined how confirming perception meets experience expectations and how disconfirming them can mean over or under-delivering. We have discussed creating awareness, working together, measuring user satisfaction, and improving digital employee experiences.

The next step will explore translating the service concept into practical plans and initiatives. We'll also uncover strategies and best practices for achieving IT satisfaction and driving business success. So, stay tuned as we continue our journey to IT satisfaction!

STEP 8. CAPTURE YOUR SERVICE CONCEPT SO YOU CAN ACT ON IT

IT satisfaction relies on collaboration between IT and the business to shape strategy, design, delivery, and operations.

How will you link your IT strategy to business agility and value? With a service concept, and let me say it right now — *service concepts are for any IT solution you provide to your internal or external partners, not just IT services!*

Fostering open communication and mutual learning with your business partners is essential. An IT service concept is a unique product or service definition with three goals. First, to define purpose in terms of results achieved rather than services performed. Next, to guide IT on what to deliver and how. And finally, understand its value equation in business terms (think BVaR).

A service concept for an IT solution focuses on delivering a positive experience to *external customers* by meeting the needs of *internal customers and users.*

What do you do for whom, why, and how?

Most IT people can't answer that question. It's fun to ask it, too, because after the giggling dies down and uncomfortable silence makes it evident that they don't know the answer, it leads to transformative conversations.

Creating a service concept asks four essential questions, without which IT won't deliver the digital experiences required for business success. It bridges the gaps between the marketplace, business, employee expectations, and what IT provides to answer four primary questions:

1. What are the capabilities of the IT solution stated in terms of value created for external customers?
2. How do internal and external customers and users perceive those IT solution capabilities?
3. How well does the service concept align with IT and business goals?
4. How must IT design, deliver, and operate to meet these requirements?

I struggled to collaborate with business partners to enhance IT satisfaction during my early career as an IT leader.

Unfortunately, a lack of feedback from the business held me back. It was a frustrating cycle where I needed business input to improve IT satisfaction but couldn't get it.

Enter the service concept, the missing piece to my IT satisfaction puzzle. I advise creating a service concept for improvements or new IT solution development.

A service concept is a document that captures the outcomes and experiences provided to IT consumers with sufficient detail to excite them. It should explain the IT solution in business terms by highlighting its value, results, and the experiences necessary to deliver it. It should avoid technical jargon (at least in the initial, condensed version you share with them).

We previously highlighted the importance of aligning IT Planning, Building, Transitioning, and Running functions. Taking it further, alignment with the business is crucial since PBTR and business functions are interconnected and interdependent.

Our next step is to collaborate and build a shared blueprint — a service concept — to drive IT satisfaction improvements.

FIGURE 8-1. Service Concept Optimized for IT Satisfaction.

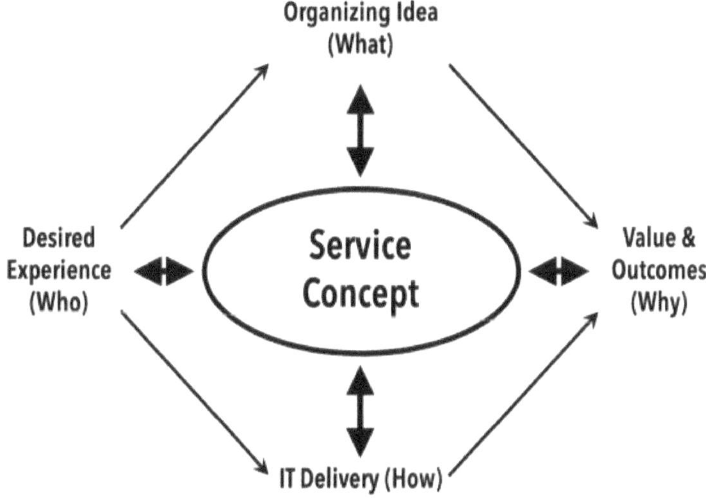

Figure 8-1, adapted from Goldstein for use in IT, shows how a service concept focuses on delivering a positive experience. It consists of four key elements that align everyone and bridges the gap between expectations and what's delivered. Working through Figure 8-1 counter-clockwise:

1. **Idea:** the essence of your IT solution, "what" it does for whom, and why at a high and non-technical level.
2. **Experience:** the workgroup and customer's direct experience of the IT solution, how it interacts with internal and external customers and users (who.)
3. **IT delivery:** your approach or "how" you'll deliver the product or service solution operationally, described in business language related to outcomes and results internal and external consumers will obtain.
4. **Value & Outcomes:** user-perceived benefits weighed against the effort or "costs" of using the solution and expressed in terms of "why" — the benefits and results your solution provides whoever uses it (internal/external user, their end-customers, your business.) BVaR can significantly influence the value and outcomes section.

These interconnected elements, represented by bidirectional arrows in Figure 8-1, signify the integration required for a cohesive and aligned IT service concept. Each component is crucial in ensuring a well-functioning and valuable IT solution.

Your service concept provides a consistent structure for developing an IT solution that meets IT consumer needs and expectations by:

- **Serving as a starting point for establishing XLA/SLA conditions** by offering a baseline for mutual expectations and requirements between IT and its consumers — internal and external.

- **Describing who will use the IT solution** in a solution-provider approach (e.g., an HR advisor helping an employee; or an employee working with a buyer in the marketplace.)
- **Capturing value and BVaR** to justify resource allocations and identify, select, and prioritize IT solutions for improvement.
- **Defining the delivery model** and providing a strategy foundation so IT plan, build, transition, and run teams can better understand how they need to interact, creating the most effective and efficient IT solution possible.

An example of a summary service concept capturing the essentials of a solution for healthcare providers who move between offices might look like this:

Service Concept Summary: *Provider Mobility Solution*

The healthcare provider mobility solution delivers a secure and easy-to-use platform (***idea, "what"***) that helps healthcare providers (***users, "internal who"***) access patient (***customers, external "who"***) data and collaborate with other professionals on the go (***experience***). The business gets lower costs, higher clinical productivity, more security, better efficiency in healthcare management, scalability, agility, and improved patient satisfaction (***value, "why"***). The solution uses identity management, encryption, authentication & authorization, data lakes, file storage, and a mobile app (***operation "how"***). This helps secure access to sensitive data and provides a friendly user interface. It also supports secure telecommunication and telemedicine (***outcomes, "why"***).

Note that in the preceding, what's important isn't a rigid structure per se. What matters is that you touch all the points.

It's okay to include as many clarifying non-technical references as you like — but don't miss any of the "big 4" shown in Figure 8-1.

For example, in Figure 8-2, you'll see the terms "workgroup" and "approaches" used to refer to those users who will directly interact with the system and the approach IT will take to deliver the solution and its value.

Neither are the "big 4" titles in the example service concept in Figure 8-2, but they're well described, so it works.

You don't need manic devotion to a formula or framework. Instead, hit all the marks, and do it in a way that works for your situation.

Figure 8-2 shows a simple template to help get you started.

FIGURE 8-2. Example Simple Service Concept Statement Template

The (<u>Idea/What</u>) is an IT solution for (<u>Experiences/Who</u>) that (<u>Workgroup/Who</u>) uses to (<u>Value/Why</u>) using (<u>Approaches/How</u>) to (<u>Outcomes/Why</u>).

Figure 8-3 is an illustrative example you could develop on a dry-erase board in a workshop using Figure 8-2 as a template.

FIGURE 8-3. Service Concept Statement Example

> Our **Customer Loyalty Application** is an IT solution for **real-time chats with customers** that **CSMs** use to **connect customers to correct products fast** using **custom software and support** to **increase CSM close rates.**

Your Winning IT Solution Experience Blueprint

By illustrating both sides of IT solution production and consumption, the service concept links IT to business outcomes. I've found a succinct "1-page service concept" document to be the most useful in facilitating discussions.

Figure 8-4 expands on the simple "concept statement" presented in Figure 8-3. An even more detailed version can also call out IT PBTR-specific functions, metrics, and other IT requirements — but you probably wouldn't share all that detail with customers and users.

FIGURE 8-4. Simplified Service Concept Template for Sharing with Business Partners

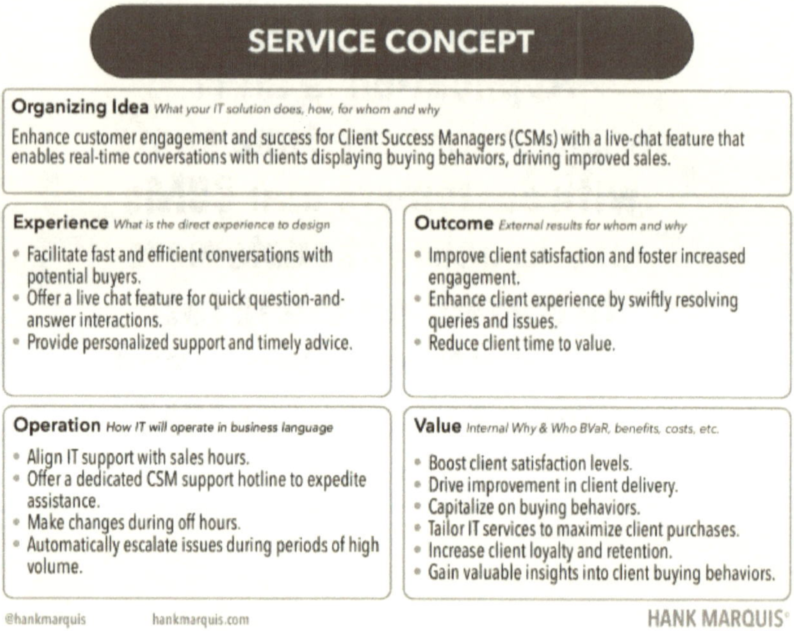

You can get the simple service concept template used in Figure 8-4 (and others) at hankmarquis.com.

Unlocking experiences & outcomes for your internal and external customers and users.

We must interact directly with users and customers to develop IT solutions. Collaboration and a user-centric approach are essential for satisfying their needs and expectations regarding IT solutions—co-creation results in happier users, improved business outcomes, and a competitive edge.

Your service concept is the tool that makes this happen. It ensures everyone is on the same page, resolves the conflict between implementation and vision, and connects end-customer needs and solution design to your company's strategic goals.

With a service concept, you can:

- **Create** organizational alignment within IT and between IT and business units,
- **Assess** the requirements and implications of solution support or delivery design changes,
- **Drive** strategic advantage with higher IT satisfaction, digital employee experience, productivity, end-customer satisfaction and loyalty, and profits.

This looks like a Service or Experience Level Agreement; we did this already!

If you have XLA/SLAs in place but don't have a service concept, this is what you're missing!

An SLA primarily defines measurable targets and responsibilities for service delivery. In contrast, an XLA takes a broader perspective by focusing on the holistic user experience (QoE), satisfaction, and value derived from IT services. The XLA is more comprehensive and includes expectations that may go beyond the simple operational (QoS) performance measurement of the SLA.

The service concept is an overarching view of the service regarding its usage, purpose, and value. It doesn't compete with the XLA/SLA but provides the key message of what to expect. The XLA/SLA, on the other hand, focuses more on giving details of expectations and outcomes. It builds off the service concept to provide more in-depth service expectations.

The XLA/SLA extends the service concept by providing more structure and detail. The XLA/SLA helps align the service delivery with expectations and ensures a positive user experience. It complements the service concept by providing specific targets and responsibilities to measure and improve service performance.

I bet you didn't do this already.

A service concept is a high-level idea or vision of the solution that an organization wants to offer to its consumers. It defines the IT solutions scope, goals, outcomes, target audience, and value proposition using outside-in business and external customer terms. It answers, "What do you do for whom, why, and how?"

Most of us get to one or two of the value points of a service concept, and I've never seen a complete one developed by any IT organization (before we start talking about it!) But Disney, for example, is famous for designing experiences — it's worked for them and will for you too.

A service concept helps guide IT development and delivery by outlining what IT must achieve and how to deliver it to meet customer needs and expectations.

In contrast, the XLA/SLA offers a measurable way to ensure that the service meets the agreed-upon standards and performance metrics it takes to deliver on the service concept.

Here's a little test for your IT strategy and design teams. If you can't answer these questions, you need a service concept!

Choose one of your IT solutions, something your team does for the business. In your next meeting with them, ask these questions about the IT solution. Better yet, try this test yourself:

1. Who is the customer (individual or organization that specifies what the solution does and often funds it) for this solution?
2. Which enterprise products or services does the IT solution underpin?
3. Which end-customers in the marketplace directly or indirectly benefit from the solution?
4. How do end-users of your enterprise benefit from the solution?
5. How do internal customers and users define value from this solution?
6. What personal motivators do users have that drive their expectations for service?
7. What are the critical primary solution characteristics — Reliability, Responsiveness, Assurance, Empathy, and Tangibles?
8. In what order of importance do the different customers rank these characteristics for their success?
9. How many workgroups (collections of people doing the same essential job functions) of the solution exist, and how many have different needs?
10. Are your plan, build, transition, and run teams aligned with each other on these questions, using the same planning documents and co-creating with customers and users?

How did you do? If you scored eight or higher out of ten, that's fantastic, and you're ready to lead your team to improve IT satisfaction. You've proven your knowledge of your business.

If you scored between 6 and 7, you did okay but likely need more preparation.

If you scored five or less, don't worry too much. You have plenty more opportunities to take the lead and develop a better strategy — and now you know what you need to study!

***

Satisfaction Story: *The Inventory System Upgrade*

Background: A logistics company faced challenges with its inventory tracking and warehouse management system, leading to decreased productivity and increased errors. Despite meeting the Service Level Agreement (SLA), warehouse staff expressed dissatisfaction. The system interface was challenging to use, hindering productivity and causing errors. The warehouse staff was unhappy, impacting overall operational efficiency.

Results: The company adopted a holistic approach to address these issues comprehensively. They implemented a service concept and metrics needed to meet the designed experience. This approach involved bringing IT and warehouse staff together to develop and align common goals. They modified the application based on the service concept, specifically catering to the needs and goals of the warehouse staff. Next, they updated their operational (SLA) and related experience (XLA) metrics.

Conclusion: The implementation of the application upgrade resulted in significant improvements. Productivity increased, errors decreased, and warehouse staff satisfaction improved. The company successfully co-created IT and business functions by meeting operational (QoS) requirements and enhancing experience (QoE), improving operational efficiency and employee satisfaction.

***

The IT Business Dance and Navigating the Challenges of IT Co-Creation

IT and business have equally important and intertwined roles in co-creation. Collaborative communication is crucial for successful IT projects. The IT organization supplies technical infrastructure and expertise, while the business provides vision, strategy, and resources.

It's not always easy, however. Sometimes you've alienated the very people you need to work with. Other times the people you need to work with won't know how to respond to your questions, especially around BVaR. But don't give up! We in IT need to lead IT satisfaction efforts.

There are many ways to get those with the information you need to share with you — and once again, the path to success will be talking about business outcomes in end-customer terms to engage them.

For example, telling the CFO you need half a million in unplanned expenses for technical debt is likely to get a very different result than asking the CFO if they want to produce 2,000 more tractors per year with a lower cost per unit (the business outcomes of that half a million ask!) Lead with the business outcomes in business terms.

Challenges in IT co-creation and how the service concept can help overcome them.

Challenges that may arise in IT co-creation include a lack of trust between IT and the business, misalignment of goals and objectives, and lacking resources.

To avoid misunderstandings, use a service concept to align IT and business perspectives and justify appropriate resources. The service concept can also help to build trust between IT and the business by providing a framework for collaboration and communication.

Use these ideas to engage your business partners by talking about the fundamental principles of the service concept:

- **Continuous collaboration between IT and business teams:** IT and business teams must work together to create solutions that meet the needs of both sides. It takes ongoing team dialogue to ensure the solutions meet all stakeholders' needs.
- **Shared vision:** IT and business teams must clearly understand the desired outcome of the IT solution. Communicate and confirm with all stakeholders to ensure everyone is on the same page.
- **Business Alignment:** The vision must align with the organization's goals and objectives.
- **Flexibility:** The Service Concept should be flexible enough to accommodate changes and stay current with the organization's needs.
- **Co-creation:** The Service Concept encourages business teams' joint ownership of IT solutions by tailoring IT to business needs and expectations.

By adopting and applying the principles of the Service Concept, IT and business teams can create solutions that meet the needs and expectations of all stakeholders. This approach to design and delivery can help organizations create successful IT solutions tailored to their specific needs.

Developing a service concept is a team effort spanning five key steps.

The service concept is an approach to developing IT solutions focusing on consumer needs and co-creating value with internal customers and users. It creates organizational alignment within IT and between IT and business units.

Lead with the service concept to co-create IT solutions. The process is understanding customer needs, creating service concepts, developing solutions, piloting the service, and managing the service.

1. **Understanding digital employee needs:** First is understanding what employees need and want and how our solutions can help them. We need to talk to them about their current situation.
2. **Creating service concepts:** Second is creating a service concept that captures the needs of our solution users. You need to uncover the services required, service levels, their value proposition, and the business model that will enable the service to be delivered. It should also provide a detailed plan for implementing the service.
3. **Developing IT solutions:** This third task involves developing the solutions needed to deliver the service concept. Selecting and integrating the necessary technologies and designing and building the solution or service, for

example. Additionally, it involves developing and testing to ensure IT meets employee and end-customer and user needs.

4. **Piloting the solution:** The fourth task involves introducing the new solution or service with limited employees to gain feedback and adjust as needed. Such tests ensure the new or improved IT solution meets needs and expectations.

5. **Managing the solutions' experience:** The last step is ensuring the new solution meets their needs. Critical operational activities include monitoring user and customer QoE feedback, addressing issues, and making necessary changes.

Enhancing IT satisfaction through collaborative service concepts.

Deliver satisfying IT solutions by communicating openly, learning from each other, and keeping users and value at the center of your leadership. The service concept helps you meet business needs and make users happy.

The service concept goes beyond operational IT metrics to focus on business value and the experiences needed to capture that value. It helps IT and business teams work together, leveraging their expertise to create IT solutions that satisfy users and customers.

Through ongoing collaboration, shared goals, and the same vision, the service concept helps create IT solutions that give your business an edge. A well-formed service concept can deliver higher IT satisfaction, better digital employee experiences, retention, productivity, end-customer satisfaction, and higher profits. Not to mention it can reduce your workload and stress levels.

This step examined why IT and business teams must work together, gave examples, and showed why using the service concept framework is a potential game changer for IT.

Now that you understand the importance of connecting IT investments to business value let's move on to understanding how and where gaps in delivery arise to fix IT satisfaction problems.

STEP 9. USE THE GAPS MODEL TO FIX DELIVERY CHALLENGES

If you've been struggling with recurring problems across one or more IT solutions, you've got a deeper problem. Here's your solution.

Resolving IT dissatisfaction with the Gaps Model answers, *"Where do missed expectations and IT delivery problems arise?"* and involves an examination of consumer expectations and IT actions.

Providing functional IT solutions is essential for any organization that wants to achieve its business objectives. As IT Leaders, we *plan*, *build* or buy to suit, *transition* the solution into production, and *run* or operate it (PBTR.)

But let's be honest — IT solution delivery can be complicated because it involves multiple teams, priorities, trade-offs, and activities. Ultimately, any dissatisfaction is a result of one or more PBTR failures.

Enter Gap analysis which connects IT dissatisfaction to misalignments between PBTR activities — so you can resolve them. In this game-changing step, you'll see how to diagnose and improve your IT organization to remove the root causes of experience failures.

IT satisfaction diagnosis and therapy!

Just as medical diagnosis helps identify the root cause of a health issue, the diagnosis of IT satisfaction problems helps identify the underlying causes of user dissatisfaction. Treatment involves organizational (people, process, products, providers) changes to address the identified issues and improve satisfaction. Therapy provides targeted interventions and support to help users overcome challenges and enhance their IT experience.

We've talked about diagnosing QoE up to this point. Now we're going to talk remediation — IT therapy!

The main difference between diagnostic and therapeutic in an IT setting is that diagnostic is the process of identifying an IT issue, while therapeutic is the process of resolving an IT issue.

Diagnostic involves troubleshooting, analysis, and observation to determine the cause of an IT issue, while therapeutic consists of a plan of action to address the issue and ensure digital employee experience and IT satisfaction.

The Gaps model does both at an IT functional level.

FIGURE 9-1. The Gaps Model

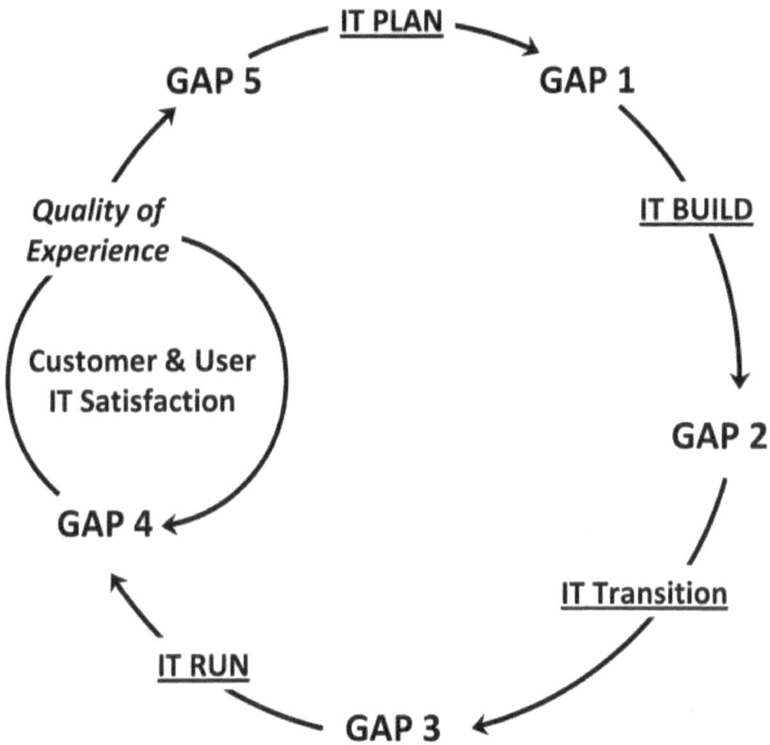

Figure 9-1 shows the five-dimensional Gaps model and how planning, building, transitioning, and running IT solutions is cyclical. PBTR missteps lead to measurable Gaps in delivery, which show up as IT dissatisfaction at Gap 5.

Use the Gaps Model to identify the gaps between IT activities and your consumers (customers and users.)

Each Gap is both diagnostic and therapeutic:

- **Gap 1:** The Knowledge or "*IT Strategy Gap*" is the difference between consumer experience expectations and IT planning leadership's understanding of them. That is, knowing what consumers expect (and need.) The IT strategic planning function owns this gap. Plan activities involve setting objectives, gathering requirements, developing tactics, and defining the scope of the effort.

- **Gap 2:** The Standards or "*IT Design Gap*" is the difference between the IT build function's understanding of consumer perceptions and documented product or service QoS and QoE engineering and support specifications. Any failures here affect the IT build function. Build-stage work comprises the proposed solution's development, sourcing, and testing.

- **Gap 3:** The Performance or "*IT Transition Gap*" is the difference between documented IT solution specifications and what gets put into production. Transition reflects the collaboration between the teams responsible for building and running the IT solution to ensure a successful and smooth implementation into production.

- **Gap 4:** The Communications or "*IT Operation Gap*" is the difference between IT solution performance and the Run teams' communications to employees about what they can expect, often due to IT Run function operations but also caused by Gaps 1-3 failures. Run actions involve the solution's administration, maintenance, and support over its lifetime.

- **Gap 5:** The Quality Gap, the difference between IT consumer expectations and their perceptions of the experience (QoE) delivered. (Gap Five is what we've been discussing up until now! Since we've covered this one, we'll focus on gaps 1-4 here.)

How to diagnose and improve your organization to determine the root cause of IT satisfaction failures.

Gap Analysis is like chiropractic or acupuncture for IT satisfaction. The Gaps model identifies blockages and information flow issues between IT consumer expectations and actual IT delivery. PBTR activities are you adjust to remediate gaps. The two models' interfaces link logically because gaps exist within and between PBTR functions.

Together, they help us assess and improve the quality of IT solutions from an IT satisfaction perspective.

Gaps are strategic. They subsume any operating model, approach, or tactic. They're also agnostic regarding your tactics or "how" you'll carry out its activities.

For example, you might favor Agile, DevOps, or DevSecOps. Or maybe something else. Your methods could be any combination of service, product, or project-oriented operating models. The Gaps model works equally well in all cases.

A word of advice: abstract your thinking to focus on Gaps because while the core IT PBTR functions don't change — IT tactics do, often regularly.

Internal factors like communication and collaboration issues between teams, insufficient skill and knowledge transfer, and inadequate change management and transition planning affect IT performance. Regardless of what you call them or who does the work, these factors are the causes of gaps between teams planning, building, transitioning, or running IT solutions.

When these activities are misaligned, it leads to inefficiencies, delays, and even project failures.

Here are some extra reasons why Gap Analysis is essential:

1. **Consistency and efficiency:** When IT PBTR functions are

aligned, the overall IT initiative has greater consistency and efficiency. The planning phase sets the foundation for the initiative, the building phase creates the solution, the transitioning phase ensures a smooth deployment, and the run phase maintains the solution. If any of these activities are misaligned or don't see eye to eye, it usually creates unnecessary rework and delays, along with IT and consumer angst.

2. **Cost-effectiveness:** Working together using a shared "blueprint" ensures cost-effectiveness by reducing the risk of cost overruns and maximizing the return on IT investments. Remember to use the ZoT and service concept here!

3. **Quality assurance:** All teams contributing to and working off a shared planning document helps to ensure that the IT initiative meets the quality standards set by the organization. When PBTR functions are not aligned, it can lead to quality issues, such as defects or inconsistencies: digital friction, and dissatisfaction.

4. **Better communication and collaboration:** Reduce the silo effect, miscommunications, and a lack of cooperation as all stakeholders work towards a common goal.

Gap Analysis for When IT Takes a Wrong Turn

Gaps analysis and the Gaps Model get us back on track when our tactics take us down the wrong path. The good news is that you can quickly and inexpensively recover and reduce or eliminate gaps — all it takes is you leading with satisfaction.

"If you think good design is expensive, you should look at the cost of bad design."

— Dr. Ralf Speth

Gap analysis pinpoints delivery disconnects between IT and its customers and users' perceptions of IT performance. Fewer and smaller gaps mean better performance for improved IT product and service experience, satisfaction, and positive quality evaluations.

As you read the coming information about the four gaps, consider how well they align with PBTR. The two management tools work hand in glove to diagnose IT faults. You'll see also that you can use them to *prevent* IT gaps from PBTR faults. You'll discover that they're interconnected — any change for any reason in any gap can cause the breakdown of your entire IT delivery chain. Problems can cascade and grow from a simple omission of strategy elements into low digital employee productivity and end-customer churn very quickly.

To drive home the point of the simple-sounding PBTR leadership advice and its criticality to IT satisfaction, the following is a Satisfaction Story about BigBrandCompany (BBC.) A failure analysis shows how quickly an IT solution can go wrong. Don't be this IT leadership team, please!

***

Satisfaction Story: *Cloud-Based Solution Implementation.*

Background: BBC is a large consulting company that struggled to find a solution to streamline its client service management platform to increase client engagement. To solve this issue, they decided to build a new cloud-based solution. The IT department faced significant challenges in delivering its solution. Errors, omissions, and failures resulted in service gaps, leading to IT dissatisfaction, disengagement, turnover, customer churn, and financial losses.

The project faced several critical gaps that impacted the successful implementation of the cloud-based solution:

- *Misalignment of Customer Expectations*: The project began with a Gap 1 failure to properly align customer expectations with management's perception. The IT department did not adequately gather comprehensive requirements, leading to a lack of clarity regarding the desired outcomes and functionality. They had no written service concept.
- *Flawed Design*: The IT department faced design challenges due to the Gap 2 misalignment in understanding customer expectations from Gap 1. The design team misinterpreted or overlooked critical requirements.
- *Execution and Delivery Problems*: The flawed design from Gap 2 delayed the execution and delivery phases of the project (Gap 3.) The IT department encountered technical and compatibility problems deploying the solution that required patching.
- *Communication Breakdown*: As problems persisted during delivery, IT mismanaged communications (Gap 4) and struggled to address concerns with internal and external users and customers.

Results:

- *Low-Quality Experience:* The cumulative effect of the preceding gaps led to a low-quality experience for end-users and external customers. The new solution didn't meet expectations.
- *IT Dissatisfaction, Disengagement, Turnover, and Financial Losses:* The failure to deliver a working solution caused internal dissatisfaction and disengagement within the IT department and the business. Frustrated employees sought opportunities elsewhere, leading to a high turnover rate. The company had financial losses due to customer churn resulting from poor quality experience and failure to meet consumer expectations.

Conclusion: The IT department failed to deliver a working cloud-based solution due to a cascade of gap failures. Misaligned expectations led to flawed design, execution problems, and recovery attempts caused communications breakdowns. Overall, a low-quality experience.

Addressing each gap is crucial to avoid such issues. By learning from these challenges, IT leadership would improve future IT projects and prioritize user and customer-centricity for successful solution implementation.

***

Over the rest of this chapter, let's unpack what went wrong, discuss how to make things right, and learn how to prevent it next time. And you can. Easily.

Bridging the Vision-Reality Divide in IT Solution Delivery

Gap 1 is the "Knowledge Gap." Its cause is a difference between IT consumer expectations and IT management perceptions of those expectations. Your IT solution's strategy must align with its internal customers' and users' needs and expectations, and that means you need to know what those two related but very different groups need to achieve to be successful.

Success at Gap 1 takes an agreed plan of action to meet QoS and QoE requirements for an IT solution's expected experiences. Gap 1 failures arise when IT plans don't capture all criteria sufficiently.

Figure 9-2 shows where the Knowledge gap fits into the IT solution lifecycle.

FIGURE 9-2. The IT Experience-to-Plan or "Knowledge" Gap

Figure 9-2 lists the primary causes of Gap 1 failures. Do you know what all parties to your IT solution — internal and external — need to be successful?

Capturing technical and experience expectations for internal and external customers and users of your IT solution strategy is challenging. But you jeopardize your build, transition, and run functions if you don't, not to mention IT satisfaction, digital employee experience, and business value.

"Knowledge is useless unless you put it into practice."

— *Anton Chekhov*

Setting the stage for IT satisfaction starts at Gap 1. Precision and accuracy are paramount. Any errors here typically cascade and magnify as they throw off the subsequent build, transition, and run functions. The result is Gap 2, 3, and 4 issues with devastating consequences for Gap 5 and digital employee experience.

Resolving and preventing Gap 1 strategy and planning errors requires increasing interactions between IT planning, customers, and users to understand and create service concepts by:

- Fostering management interaction with IT consumers (IT and business customers and users.)
- Conducting systematic research into IT customer and user value, experience, and satisfaction needs.
- Using research results effectively and sharing them with PBTR teams.
- Encouraging unfiltered upward communication from IT consumer-contact employees.

The following Satisfaction Story shows how faulty or incomplete strategy causes problems down the PBTR line.

***

Satisfaction Story: *Fixing Knowledge Gap*

Background: BBC thought a new cloud-based IT solution would enhance productivity. They didn't have a service concept, so their strategy engagement efforts primarily focused on the CIO capturing the customer's (business function leader's) goals and neglecting to understand the goals and requirements of the users (digital employees.) The project began with a Gap 1 failure because the CIO didn't include all stakeholder's users' specific objectives and needs, including internal and external roles.

Results: To recover, IT held interviews and hosted workshops. They utilized prototyping and design tools to create interactive prototypes and mock-ups. They implemented a change management system and used impact assessment templates to track and manage change requests. They relied on project management and collaboration platforms for feedback sessions, demos, and updates to maintain continuous consumer engagement.

Conclusion: By taking a prosumer-centric approach and involving users in addition to customers in the IT strategy and planning process, they created a service concept. They closed Gap 1 and ensured that their IT initiatives met the needs and expectations of all stakeholders.

***

Closing the Knowledge Gap requires a service concept, effective communication, employee involvement, feedback mechanisms, easy-to-understand performance agreements, a satisfaction-centric culture, a continuous improvement mindset, and investment in IT employee training and development:

- **Plan:** Work with employees to flesh out a prosumer-centric IT strategy for each solution. Using RATER, conduct surveys, focus groups, and other methods to gather internal customer and user feedback on their needs and expectations for IT services.
- **Do:** Analyze the data to identify common themes and pain points and prioritize them based on their impact on user IT satisfaction and business outcomes.
- **Check:** Use the feedback and analysis to inform IT strategy and planning decisions, update or create your service concept, and ensure that they all align with each stakeholder's needs and expectations (internal and external.)

- **Act:** Communicate the IT strategy and planning decisions to internal customers and users, highlighting how the strategy addresses their joint needs and expectations.
- **Monitor and adjust:** Review all feedback and adjust your IT strategy and planning decisions regularly to ensure they align with expectations.

Designing IT Solutions that Satisfy

The gap between IT management perceptions of consumer expectations (Gap 5), strategy planning at Gap 1, and IT solution specifications is Gap 2. This "Standards Gap" pertains to IT solution planning and design. Building a successful IT solution requires an IT design team that fully understands its customers' and users' needs and expectations to deliver adequate IT solution specifications.

> "It is useful to think about design as a process of communication among various audiences."
>
> — *Thomas Erickson*

Problems arise at Gap 2 when designers and engineers don't have or understand IT fully solution QoS and QoE requirements or ignore them because of costs or other constraints.

Figure 9-3 shows the location of the Standards gap in the lifecycle of a solution.

FIGURE 9-3. The IT Plan-to-Build or "Standards" Gap

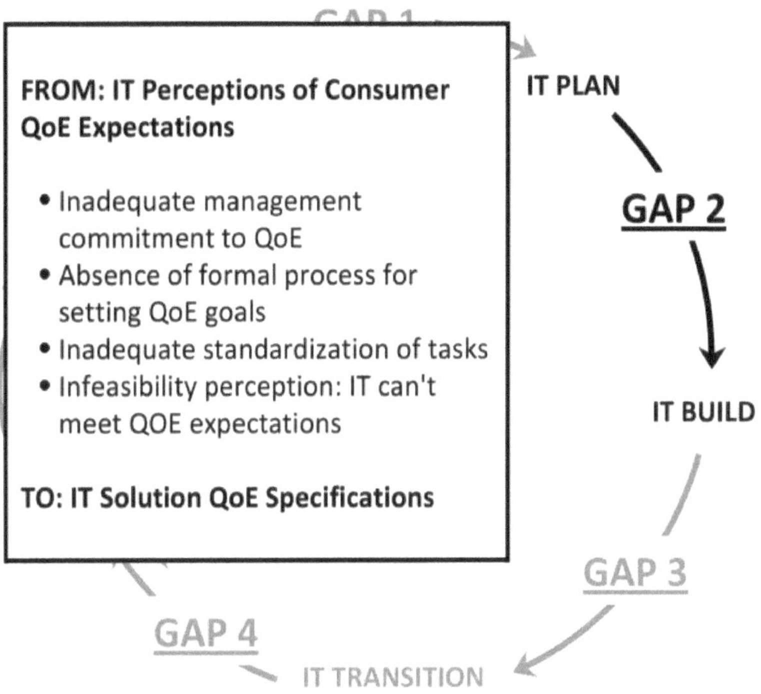

Figure 9-3 lists the causes of Gap 2 failures. Do you view design as a communication process among various audiences? If you want to deliver IT solutions that satisfy, then you need to! Translation of strategy expectations into IT solution quality specifications is Gap 2, the "Standards Gap," and it's a team sport.

To improve or recover at Gap 2 (Build) after closing Gap 1 (Plan) requires practical and functional service design processes for:

- A completed, co-created service concept.
- Participation in IT strategy and planning activities.
- Management commitment to IT satisfaction (aka, leading with satisfaction!)
- Formal goal-setting methods for IT solution experience.

- Eliminating perceptions of infeasibility through management commitment and support.
- Task standardization — the design must account for the work that others must do, as well as expected behaviors and automation for repetitive tasks to ensure experience consistency.

***

Satisfaction Story: *Closing the Standards Gap*

Background: BBC's IT strategy lacked the inclusion of critical elements required to address the specific goals and needs of the users. Due to the incomplete strategy, the design team lacked a clear understanding of business requirements and omitted critical IT solution capabilities. They built a solution that couldn't fully meet user expectations. They needed to align the new management perceptions of the cloud tool quality specifications, ensuring consistent and satisfactory delivery to meet stakeholder expectations.

Approach: They implemented solution design and standardization and developed a service concept using tools like Service Blueprinting and Value Stream Mapping. They defined clear service standards and specifications. They also focused on XLA/SLA performance measurement using KPIs and monitoring systems for QoS and QoE. They worked with Human Resources to design comprehensive training programs to empower employees. They created a Cloud Satisfaction Team, efficient complaint-handling processes, and feedback management systems for Run teams. With this approach — and accurate data from the IT Plan function — they completed the service concept and passed the QoS, QoE, and implementation information to IT Transition.

Results: To close this gap, they ensured that the IT solutions' specifications accurately reflected internal customers' and users' needs and expectations for QoE and QoS. Solving this problem took a service concept project, effective communication, and collaboration between IT Plan and Build.

***

To bridge the Standards Gap 2, prioritize customer-centricity, gather accurate requirements, ensure coordination, allocate resources, and continuously review and improve specifications based on IT user and customer feedback and their evolving needs as follows:

- **Plan:** Understand solution expectations. Use feedback to know what internal and external customers and users need and expect from the IT solution.
- **Do:** Translate IT Plan experience expectations into quality specifications. Turn workplace and outcome expectations into clear and specific technical and quality specifications, ensuring they accurately reflect all stakeholders.
- **Check:** Communicate the QoS and QoE specifications to stakeholders, including IT staff, internal customers and users, and management, to ensure alignment with everyone on the expected IT experience quality.
- **Act:** Ensure that IT solution quality specifications, as determined through monitoring and measurement and regular feedback from internal customers and users, makes it into your strategy process.
- **Monitor:** Continuously improve design quality. Use feedback from customers and users to continuously improve designs, ensuring they remain aligned with current (and future) needs and expectations.

Smoothly Transitioning IT Solutions from Design to Operations

Gap 3 refers to any differences between IT solution quality specifications from Gap 2 and the solution's production performance. Success at the "Performance Gap" is aligning IT transition to production and delivery functions with engineering blueprints from the IT build function.

> "The best laid schemes o' Mice an' Men Gang aft agley, An' lea'e us nought but grief an' pain."
>
> — *Robert Burns*

Problems at Gap 3 often come from poor design (Standard and Knowledge Gaps) and surface when there are mismatches between the expected and actual IT solution delivery due to people, process, and partner problems that make it difficult for delivery staff to deliver to specifications.

Figure 9-4 positions the Performance gap in the IT solution lifecycle.

FIGURE 9-4. The IT Build-to-Transition or "Performance" Gap

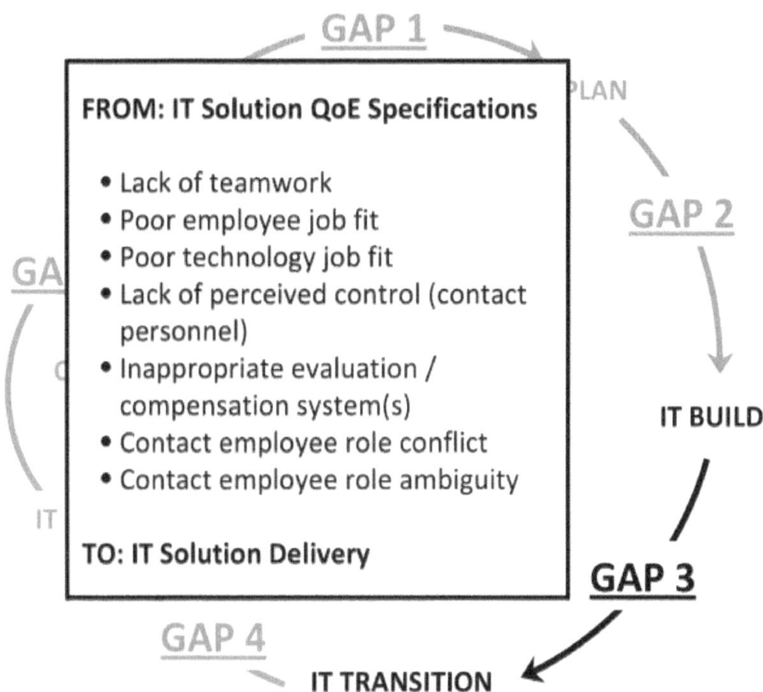

Figure 9-4 shows the causes of Gap 3 issues. Notice how most of its reasons are simple failures of IT leadership. If you've ever designed and built what you feel is an attractive IT solution that none of your customers and users liked, you know first-hand what Gap 3 is all about!

Gap 3 factors include failures of IT Plan and Build functions (Gap 1 or Gap 2 failures), inability to place and empower the correct people, processes, partners, and products into position, and delivery staff unwilling or unable to deliver to specifications.

Fix IT delivery performance (Gap 3) problems by:

- Clearing defining roles and responsibilities.
- Removing role conflict and ambiguity.
- Matching employee job and technology fit.

- Recognizing and rewarding employees who deliver superior service.
- Giving customer-contact employees sufficient flexibility.
- Building teams and fomenting teamwork.

***

Satisfaction Story: *The Performance Problem*

Background: IT had built a solution that couldn't meet user expectations. To improve delivery, IT aimed to implement the revised solution by adhering closely to its quality specifications and keeping an open conversation with IT Design and Plan functions, customers, and users.

Results: IT transition leaders focused on implementing standardized processes and workflows, utilizing tools for workflow and task management. They defined ongoing performance monitoring mechanisms and feedback loops to track service delivery and capture consumer insights. They worked with IT audit and compliance to define regular checks to ensure adherence to the quality specifications supported by quality management tools and techniques. Through this approach, they determined how to align solution delivery with quality specifications and provide consistent, high-quality experiences that meet stakeholder expectations.

Conclusion: By effectively implementing planning, testing, and monitoring the IT solution delivery process, along with partnering with IT compliance, they closed Gap 3 and set the stage for IT Run to manage the new cloud solution successfully.

***

To fix Gap 3, allocate sufficient resources and take these actions to ensure reliable and up-to-date technology infrastructure, and actively seek and respond to employee feedback while managing their expectations effectively:

- **Plan:** Well before the hand-off to operations, develop a comprehensive plan for transitioning and delivering IT solutions, including a timeline and process for testing and monitoring quality.
- **Do:** Test quality (QoS and QoE). Conduct rigorous IT operational quality and experience testing to confirm that the solution meets agreed-upon specifications.
- **Check:** Monitor delivery. Review operational metrics and experience key performance indicators regularly. Compare them to the service concept, blueprint, or design.
- **Act:** Take corrective action if delays or errors impact QoS and QoE. Address deviations from design issues and ensure that experience quality can occur as intended.
- **Monitor:** Continuously evaluate delivery quality. Use IT delivery staff feedback to assess and align the solution's performance with business needs.

Closing the Loop by Doing What You Said You Would Do

Gap 4 represents the gap between IT solution delivery, promises, and communication to customers and users about what they could expect. Consistency between what the IT organization says it will do and what delivery teams can do defines successful IT transitions to production and the Communication Gap.

"No good deed goes unpunished."

— St. Thomas Aquinas

Ongoing support and delivery require consistent communication and adherence to specifications. If there is a mismatch between what IT delivers and what they communicate or promise, digital employees will be dissatisfied. Welcome to the "Communication" Gap, #4.

For example, telling users they'll get a call back from the IT Service Desk (ITSD) within five minutes without adequately planning and allocating sufficient ITSD resources to achieve that response time. (Remember the Zone of Tolerance here, too — over-delivery can be worse than under-delivery.) Figure 9-5 shows how the IT Run function is where "the rubber meets the road" regarding completely satisfying your IT customers and users (or not.)

FIGURE 9-5. The IT Transition-to-Run or "Communication" Gap

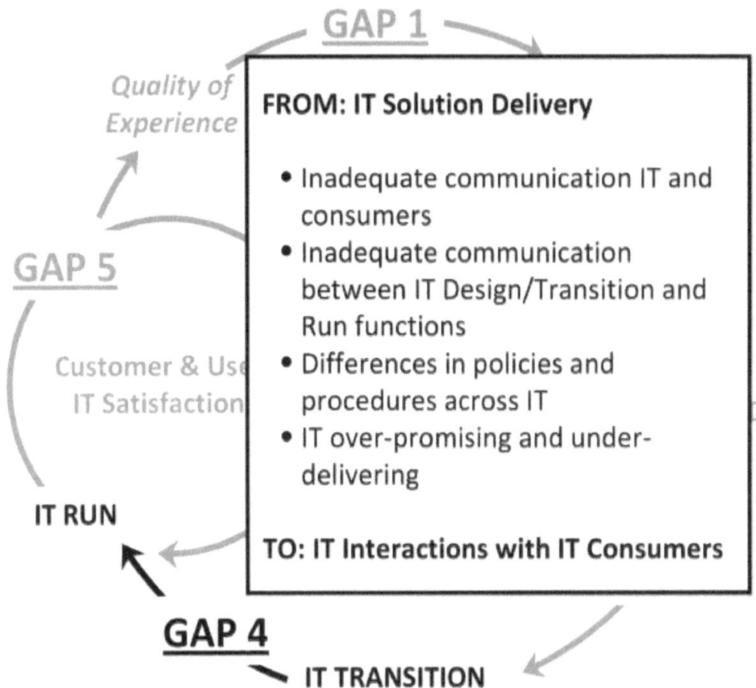

Thomas Aquinas' adage was never truer than with Gap 4, as Figure 9-5 highlights. Still, over-delivering is often a mistake for IT because it implies a new delivery promise!

Causes of Gap 4 Operation failures also include Gap 1, 2, or 3 failures along with miscommunication about what customers and users can expect, not delivering as either promised or implied, mixed messages between IT groups, differences in policies and procedures across IT departments or user groups, and the propensity of IT to "over-promise."

Solving Gap 4 requires:

- Accurate communication artifacts include service catalogs, XLAs & SLAs, and standard operating procedures (SOPs) derived from your service concept within and between IT and business units.

- Consistent IT and solution-related policies and procedures across branches or departments, including IT security policies, change management procedures, standardized documentation, and communication practices.
- Management support for resisting the temptation to promise more than IT can deliver.
- Consistently delivering as a team what you promise as a team.

***

Satisfaction Story: *The Communications Gap*

Background: Users were dissatisfied with the new cloud solution because it didn't work as quickly and easily as IT had promised. Sales leadership had revised quotas upward based on IT promises, but sales users couldn't meet their quotas with the new tool. IT had to bridge the gap between the cloud solutions' promises and capabilities without over-delivering to meet users' requirements as compensation for solution inadequacies.

Results: The Run team acknowledged and owned the problem. They focused on clear and consistent communication strategies, conveying the solutions' benefits across multiple channels. The IT satisfaction team implemented additional customer feedback mechanisms and surveys to gather insights and improve service. They set up efficient processes for service recovery and complaint resolution to prioritize timely and empathetic responses. They even integrated with marketing to gain access to reputation management results from monitoring social media platforms for unhappy end-customers.

Results: IT did what it said it would. By effectively planning, testing, and monitoring the IT service delivery process, organizations closed Gap 4 and ensured they delivered their IT initiatives with the intended service quality.

***

Closing the Communications Gap is about saying what you will do and then doing that — nothing more and nothing less (within reason.)

Bridge Gap 4 with accurate and transparent communications with customers and users, maintaining consistency across communications channels, providing clear guidelines and education, delivering excellent support services, proactively communicating updates, and establishing effective feedback and complaint-handling processes.

Organizations can minimize the gap between IT solution delivery and external communication by addressing these factors, improving IT satisfaction and perceived QoE.

Be sure to tackle Gap 4 problems using PDCA:

- **Plan:** Outline how to engage digital employees affected by an IT solution, including its features, functionality, and benefits.
- **Do:** Begin communicating with your IT consumers early in the delivery process, and continue to share to ensure they're informed and engaged. Remember to do what you tell them you will!
- **Check:** Ask for insights, needs, wants, etc., throughout the delivery process to identify any gaps in communication or misunderstanding about the IT solution.
- **Act:** Offer training and support to ensure customers and

users have the knowledge and skills to use the new or changed IT solution effectively — note that those two groups usually have different needs!

- **Monitor:** Use internal feedback to improve communication about the IT solution continuously.

By effectively communicating throughout the IT PBTR process, you can close Gap 4 and ensure that you deliver IT initiatives with clear and effective communication about its features, functionality, and benefits.

Deliver Exceptional IT Solutions

Providing great IT can be complicated by multiple teams. Without stringent planning, interdependent tasks often lead to misalignment and gaps, which can cause inefficiencies, delays, and breakdowns, as we've seen.

Involve users in the IT strategy and planning process to close gaps and ensure your IT initiatives meet the needs and expectations of your business. Doing so improves digital employee experience, customer satisfaction, and business results.

Figure 9-6 summarizes the preceding four gaps. The solution to any IT QoE or satisfaction problem you have (or will have!) is within the four bullet points of Gap #5.

FIGURE 9-6. The "Quality of Experience" Gap

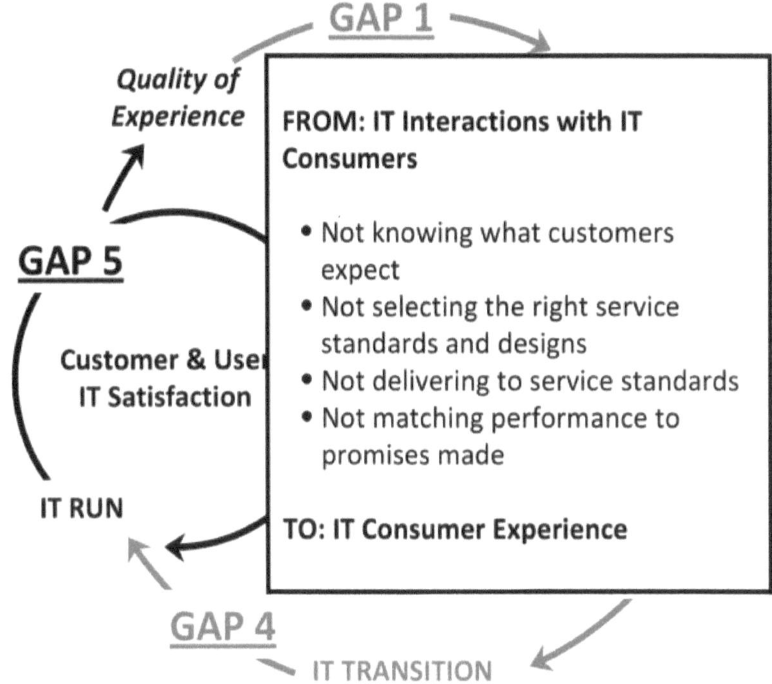

Your roadmap to exceptional IT delivery.

The Gaps Model provides a comprehensive and systematic approach to improving IT service delivery and ensuring IT consumer satisfaction.

We've seen in this step a model that emphasizes the importance of:

- Proactively understanding and addressing the needs and expectations of IT consumers.
- Translating those expectations into specific quality specifications.
- Continuously evaluating and improving IT delivery based on feedback.

By doing so, organizations can ensure that their IT strategies align with corporate goals and that their IT services consistently meet the highest levels of quality and satisfaction.

Let's move on to the next step and discuss connecting experience to company goals. We'll examine what we can do to ensure IT services support business objectives and bring value.

STEP 10. CONNECT EXPERIENCE TO COMPANY GOALS

Reducing digital friction is essential, but what excites business leaders is how IT investments drive tangible business outcomes.

Once you understand expectations, perceptions, and experiences, you'll get the best results if you justify your projects in business outcome terms. The good news is that by this point, you know them! We have to learn to speak business if we want to win.

IT improvements like "interface updates" and "networking upgrades" can lead to benefits such as "easier to use" and "supporting chatbots." But to get IT funding to make those improvements, you must connect benefits to business value using business terms.

In this step, you'll capture the value your IT improvements enable for your company. We'll determine business value and how to communicate it in business terms.

For example, in the Financial Services industry, the business value could be "increasing client satisfaction while reducing costs and fraud rates."

For Transportation and Logistics, the value might be "improving delivery speed and accuracy while decreasing shipment damage rates."

And in Higher Education, perhaps "increasing student success rates by reducing dropouts."

No more 9's, please!

IT improvements enable benefits, which you must translate into business value in the language of your industry.

Every IT solution — from digital workplaces to infrastructure to applications and operations —contributes to or detracts from value. Each solution often provides multiple benefits, and the collection of the benefits also provides business value.

For example, IT often represents the quality of their delivery by discussing the number of "9's" of availability to state the obvious (to us!) that "more uptime" equals "more business." I hope by now you see the error of that approach!

Most business people — by definition — cannot connect the dots from IT improvements through benefits and into business value in their market segments. If you were to tell an average business customer that you were adding one more 9 to your availability, most likely they'd say, "So what, why do we need to do that, and how is this going to cost me?"

"Tell me about my lawn, not your grass seeds."

— *Unknown marketeer*

While IT has trained its customers that "more 9's are better", most business people don't see IT adding value beyond being there (aka "availability.") That's a problem, partly because most IT people have only vague ideas of how end-customers interact with the solutions they build and partly because they have little idea what it takes to work with those end-customers.

In the preceding example of the "9s", we talked about the improvement and higher availability. But we never mentioned benefits, so we can't show business value in business terms.

Instead, we need to think about the work we did for digital employee experience. We must consider how those RATER improvements affected that IT Solution and its users. Then we need to understand how they use that Solution to deliver benefits into our marketplace. Finally, that's what you must lead with when talking to your business leaders!

Table 10-1 provides a framework for demonstrating how an improvement enhances IT satisfaction, enabling specific benefits for the business and connecting to company goals.

TABLE 10-1. Business Value Justification Template

Improvement:	*Something that improves IT satisfaction*
Benefit:	*What the improvement enables for the business*
Business Value:	*How this improvement connects to a company goal or problem*
Equivalent Value:	*Translation of the business value into production counts*

Table 10-2 is a completed example of a package delivery company, where an average driver makes 120 deliveries daily but must spend about 2 hours handling damaged returns.

The cause of the damaged packages is getting crushed due to failures of the truck loading application, resulting from networking problems (technical debt causing crashes intermittently.)

TABLE 10-2. Example Business Justification for IT Technical Debt Remediation

Improvement:	Networking upgrades.
Benefit:	Better package loading.
Business Value:	Improving delivery speed and accuracy while decreasing shipment damage rates.
Equivalent Value:	It's like each driver getting 2 extra hours per day, or the ability to deliver about 15-30 more packages per driver.

Compare the example in Table 10-2 to talking about "technical debt" and "more 9's of availability".

Here's a pro tip: start backward with the template when talking to business people! Using Figure 10-2, you'd lead with something along the lines of the following: *"I've identified a way to give drivers the equivalent of 2 more hours per day, which could lead to a 10-15% uplift in packages delivered per driver — as it cuts costs."*

Moving from "improvements" to "benefits" to "business value" and then "equivalent value" often confuses IT people because they seldom see or use the unique solutions they build. To these highly dedicated and specialized IT workers, the value of what they do is intrinsic but not something they usually think about due to the distance between the data center and the front-line sales team making client calls.

Struggling for IT funding and the business outcome connection.

As an IT leader, you can find yourself in a tight spot when getting funding for IT projects essential for improving operational efficiency. For example, as an IT leader, you might have "technical debt" from older, less reliable networking equipment. Your operational QoS metrics show that availability is falling. You know you need to invest in upgrading the network.

You tried discussing how old and complex the equipment is to maintain, but the CFO denied your funding request. You then took it to the next level and explained the interdependency of applications and your networking equipment. But again, the CFO rejected your request.

Here's why: you couldn't explain what that interdependency meant in business terms. Without a clear explanation of the positive impact of your IT solution in using business outcomes that everyone can understand, the board is unlikely to approve it.

Here's a Satisfaction Story example of explaining in business terms. The first time I did this, I was shocked at how well it worked!

***

Satisfaction Story: *Accelerating Checkout*

Background: Reducing the total call at a pharmacy chain proved critical in gaining a competitive edge.

However, implementing this improvement wasn't easy. The IT team had identified the potential cost savings but faced difficulty convincing the board to fund the necessary upgrades.

Initially, the CFO hesitated to invest in the upgrade as he was unsure of its benefits. In the meeting, he said, "No. There is no budget for more IT."

We needed to communicate the business value of faster credit card transaction processing so the CFO could understand it. We put together a new presentation without any technical details. It was 100% business-centric.

We even took it further by showing how the return on investment sped up checkouts and was like "adding an extra register per pharmacy" with any added costs.

Results: At the next meeting with the CFO using the new deck, the CFO stopped our presentation on the second slide and, frowning, asked, "Who's responsible for this not happening yet?" Then, smiling, the CFO asked, "If I give you more money, can you do it sooner?"

In business terms, we had shown how removing one billing increment would accelerate sales per register, decrease costs, improve customer satisfaction, and give the pharmacy chain a competitive edge.

Why did this approach work? Because we provided the decision maker with the information they could understand in their language in non-technical business terms and outcomes. **By linking IT metrics and investments to better business outcomes, such as improved customer satisfaction and a competitive edge, we secured funding for the necessary upgrades.**

We demonstrated how reducing the total call time by one billing increment would increase sales per register and thus reduce the costs of goods sold. **This improvement would decrease operational costs as it enhanced end-customer satisfaction.**

Conclusion: Instead of talking about networking, we spoke about top-line revenue. By emphasizing the positive impact on business outcomes and aligning the proposed IT investments with the chain's strategic goals, we successfully convinced the CFO to provide additional funding. Clarifying and using business terms secured the necessary resources to implement the networking upgrades and achieve the desired results.

***

The 'why' and 'how' of justifying IT investments for improved digital employee experience using Business Value at Risk.

Once you've identified *what* it takes to improve digital employee experience, you must show business leaders *how* your IT solutions can deliver for the company. While reducing friction is important, what truly matters to them is the value your IT solution can provide.

Time and again, I've seen brilliant IT leaders falter when connecting IT to business goals. It's essential to communicate the business value of IT investments, so prioritize improvements and justify investments by linking your IT solutions ("how") to business value ("why").

BVaR clarifies what IT ought to do, how well to do it, and how much to do — in business terms. Using business instead of tech terms identifies and justifies optimizing those IT solutions. The result is built-in business-IT alignment and nearly instant payback with visible and measurable improvements in IT quality and business process performance.

Developing a sound understanding of the value of your IT solutions — in terms of the business value at risk — positions you squarely in the shoes of your consumer. Use this new understanding of quality as the basis for your communications with the business.

Of course, it also forms the basis for solution delivery, operation, and quality management activities! Discuss BVaR with senior leaders, business people, and non-IT staff about funding your IT initiatives.

For example, imagine your company uses a custom inventory management system. If that system were to go down, the business would lose the ability to track inventory levels and shipments, which could result in lost sales and unhappy end-customers.

By understanding the BVaR associated with this system, you can prioritize improvements that reduce the risk of downtime or data loss, such as implementing a backup system or upgrading hardware.

> "Destiny is no matter of chance. It is a matter of choice. It is not a thing to be waited for, it is a thing to be achieved."

> — *William Jennings Bryan*

Finally, remember that BVaR exercises are to prioritize the most critical IT improvements.

We're talking about justifying projects that can cost millions. When running a BVaR exercise, we aim to provide the most transparency possible using business metrics, terms, and situations to describe what we want to do and why.

We must cut through the chatter for your most significant initiatives to determine what matters most to your company. Don't forget that you can use the same approach to understand the BVaR for being outside the ZoT, too!

The Rx for IT success is a dose of industry insight.

Showing the business value at risk and justifying IT investments will help you get the necessary resources to improve IT satisfaction.

Understand your industry and its business objectives to justify your IT satisfaction improvements by taking the following actions:

- **Know how your business makes money or serves your constituents:** re-learn the goals and priorities of your sector. It could be finance, transport, logistics, education, or another business function. Your corporate filings and marketing are great places to start.
- **Identify IT improvements:** Look at everything from a solutions' user interface to its networking. Think about how not having what you're proposing can hurt the business. Find the areas where you can make the most significant difference in business outcomes.
- **Translate benefits to business value:** Connect IT improvements to business outcomes. Focus on the IT solution's effects on actual business results. Explain how they help reach your company's goals in the same words and metrics sales, marketing, and other business units use.
- **Speak the language of your industry:** Avoid using technical jargon when you talk to business leaders and people who don't work in IT. Speak in terms that make sense to those you're talking to.
- **Quantify the risks and benefits:** Understand the risks of IT "technical debt" — old systems and infrastructure. Figure out the advantages of investing in IT. Show how these advancements can help keep risks away, make operations faster, lower costs, and increase revenue. Then, show how your solution delivers "the equivalent of" so many new customers, students, or whatever your industry uses as its benchmark metric of success.

- **Craft compelling stories:** Creating satisfaction stories is a great way to show the value of your investments. You should focus on how IT improvements have helped your company, now and in the past. Your stories should demonstrate tangible business outcomes. Show how IT investments have had a positive impact on the bottom line. Give clear examples of how IT changes have improved operations, increased productivity, and saved money. You can make a strong case for future IT funding through your satisfaction stories.

A successful IT strategy starts with having a business-centric mindset. Speak to your business partners in a language they understand, and use their metrics to quantify the value of IT improvements.

Explain how IT investments align with the company objectives. Doing this will demonstrate the importance of IT and can secure the required funding.

With these tools, you can create your IT strategy. By following the approach outlined in this step, you can demonstrate the value of IT investments in a way that resonates with business leaders and non-IT staff.

We've covered a lot, but we're only getting started! Next, let's see what comes after you get a grip on your IT satisfaction.

EXPERIENCE SATISFACTION IN ACTION

AFTER THE STEPS, WHAT'S NEXT?

After wrapping up the service concept step of a 5-step satisfaction process workshop, many ask, "Okay, how can we improve IT satisfaction then?" To which I reply, "That's not our goal!"

Focus your attention on both your customer and user experience. Not the IT experience. We're not out to improve IT satisfaction. An IT satisfaction exercise is helpful as it aligns IT and business. But its purpose isn't to enhance IT satisfaction. That's too narrow and self-centered.

No, our goal is to improve business outcomes by removing digital friction. Remember, IT satisfaction is a lagging indicator of how well our employees can complete their jobs. We must concentrate on removing digital friction per the service concept.

Recognizing that customers and users have distinct needs and expectations is crucial and where you should start. Tailoring the measurement approach for each workgroup — and being sure to combine like workgroups — is essential.

Here's why a one-size-fits-all approach falls short.

- **Customers, such as VPs of Sales or Marketing Directors, have a strategic perspective.** They expect IT initiatives to impact departmental performance and overall business outcomes. Customer IT satisfaction focuses on aligning IT solutions with strategic objectives and aspects like business impact, strategic alignment, and clear communication. NPS is a better tool for this audience.

- **On the other hand, users are business unit employees who rely on IT solutions to perform their tasks.** Their IT satisfaction centers on balancing experience and productivity. Users often care more about simplifying their work, reliability, responsiveness, support, and training. CES is likely going to provide more insights into this audience.

To improve digital employee experience (and fix IT satisfaction problems), you must investigate digital employee experience and examine IT processes and technology to identify areas where we can reduce or remove digital friction to produce positive results.

Where to Start Improving Digital Employee Experience

If you manage IT products or services, your answers to five simple-sounding questions can help determine whether you're meeting consumer expectations. If your answer is "no" or "I don't know" to any of the five, your customers and users are likely dissatisfied with your service:

- If you're in corporate IT, this dissatisfaction means your IT solution is, at best, a nuisance and, at worst, contributing to corporate failure.
- If you're a cloud provider, you're losing business to your competition.
- Nonprofits and governmental IT organizations are wasting

money.

These five questions represent state-of-the-art thinking in digital employee experience — the formal science of managing services, particularly managing by employee and customer expectations.

You undoubtedly have at least one product, service, or solution that doesn't meet customer or user expectations for quality or value. Begin here by reviewing (or creating) the BVaR and service concept for the solution.

Choose an IT solution with performance concerns, then follow this informal verbal gap analysis.

Ask the people involved, especially your direct reports who are farther from the front lines of delivery, the following questions:

1. **Do you have a plan of action to meet digital employee expectations for the five RATER determinants?** Ask for each factor's written plan and the documented service levels required. Find out if there's a service concept in place, and if not, get it done!

2. **Have you blueprinted IT solution standards to meet each quality aspect?** Confirm that the blueprint includes this solution's people, processes, products, and partners — a complete service concept. It identifies how each one must change and to what degree to meet your plan. It should include job descriptions, new roles, process changes, automation, and related components.

3. **Were people, processes, partners, and products implemented as blueprinted?** Verify that it happened — tough to do without no. 2 above, but check the results if you have a written plan and a blueprint.

4. **Do the systems and people put in place deliver to defined**

standards? Validate that you have the means to measure your teams' performance against the new requirements. These new requirements must align with employee development and compensation systems.

5. **Are communications to customers about service quality standards correct?** Ensure you're delivering what you promised and what the customer expected, and ensure the customer's perception matches yours and that delivery staff have what they need to meet expectations.

I hope you recognized the Gaps Model in the preceding steps! Those questions imply that you can relate employee perceptions with expectations. If you can't, your customers are likely dissatisfied, and this is where to start improving your DEX.

Lead with satisfaction by asking about the solution regularly. Ask to see your team's artifacts. Make it a part of your leadership 1:1's. Talk about it at town halls.

How to Put Your IT Experience Satisfaction Service Concept into Action

To measure customer and user IT satisfaction accurately, adopt an approach based on your customers and their users' unique needs by:

- Conducting separate surveys for customers and users to gather targeted feedback and insights.
- Defining KPIs that map to customer and user IT satisfaction, such as business impact and ease of use.
- Implementing different channels for customers and users to provide feedback on their IT experiences.

IT satisfaction is a lagging indicator of success, and we must stop treating it as a leading indicator!

Leading indicators foretell the future. Lagging indicators confirm the past. IT satisfaction is a lagging indicator because it represents user evaluation of past experiences. Low IT satisfaction is a symptom, not the cause. This is important because it means IT satisfaction is a by-product. To improve IT satisfaction, you need leading metrics for the causes of dissatisfaction.

Once you identify digital friction points, you can create solutions to reduce them.

After implementing those solutions, measuring their impact on customer results rather than IT satisfaction is essential. The goal should be to measure users' quality of experience.

If QoE is "in the zone," user experience, digital employees' productivity, and engagement all increase, and IT satisfaction and business results will follow.

Which invariably leads us back to operational metrics, XLAs, and SLAs. These constructs are important to improving IT satisfaction — but only helpful in the 10-step experience satisfaction process context. Neither alone gets the job done. Together, the job gets done with fantastic effectiveness and outcomes.

Now that you're leading with satisfaction, here is how you make it go to work for you:

- Choose an IT solution to evaluate.
- Build an experience evaluation goal.
- Identify user expectations.

- Position delivery in the Zone of Tolerance.
- Develop QoE and QoS specifications.
- Communicate with customers and users.
- Make changes to operational technology.
- Monitor delivery and performance.
- Measure QoE, and repeat.

Choose an IT solution to evaluate.

This area is where getting to know your internal customers and users can make things evident you would have never thought about. Think about the Liberty Mutual example. They changed the IT maintenance window to accommodate external customer preferences. They wouldn't have known if they hadn't spent time talking to contact personnel.

Build a practical digital employee experience by completing the experience evaluation goal worksheet.

We start here when I run IT experience satisfaction workshops. A DEX goal statement is vital for targeting digital friction to increase digital employee productivity and improve experience.

Your DEX goal is a statement capturing the overarching objective or purpose that you want to achieve. You, your team, and anyone else involved must have the same understanding of this goal. I advise that you follow a very rigid structure for developing this statement. You will most likely not get the desired results if it doesn't.

It has five critical parts clearly stating what you intend to analyze, improve, or develop. They are in terms of object, purpose, and focus, and they must capture the context and the stakeholders. This leads you to which levers to pull to move your delivery into a specific user group's Zone of Tolerance.

I use a variation of the Goal-Question-Metric (GQM) method developed by Basili and Henry and piloted at the NASA Goddard Space Flight Center. If it's good enough for NASA, it's good enough for me!

Table III-1 shows five fields that form the core of a clear goal statement.

Table III-1. Experience Evaluation Goal Parts

Field	Description	Example [a]
Object	To what the evaluation applies.	Product, service, process, resource, etc.
Purpose	Reason for the evaluation.	Characterize, understand, control, improve, etc.
Focus	Quality or experience issue or area to evaluate.	Engineering, support, fitness for use or purpose, etc.
Context	Description of environment.	Using, building, supporting, administering, etc.
Stakeholder	The point of view to examine.	Customer, user, team, manager, etc.

[a] Use any word that fits your case. Even words not on these lists.

Now, combine the fields into a sentence structure as follows:

Analyze **Object** to **Purpose** the impact of **Focus** when **Context** from the viewpoint of **Stakeholder**.

Imagine you're with your Satisfaction Team. You've discovered that Responsiveness and Tangibles are the problems affecting a group of developers who use the software source code management application called "DTQ Archive." You're at a dry-erase board, and the exercise is to complete the template as shown in Figure III-1.

Figure III-1. Well-formed Experience Evaluation Statement

Analyze **DTQ Archive** to **understand** the impact of **ease and speed-of-use** when **recreating a prior version** from the viewpoint of **Application Developers**.

You'll use your goal statement throughout the 10-step process. It'll keep your satisfaction team zeroed in and help you avoid distractions. It enhances goal clarity, alignment, measurability, focus, and decision-making. It fosters a culture of continuous improvement and is essential for you to establish meaningful, attainable goals and monitor progress toward desired outcomes.

Leading IT Satisfaction

When I lead IT satisfaction or improvement efforts and workshops, here's the approach I follow or demonstrate. Adapt the following to fit your need, of course, and note that this doesn't have to take months or quarters to accomplish either!

Identify workgroup expectations.

The IT satisfaction team must identify user or customer expectations for a specific IT solution, like the preceding DTQ example, provided by corporate IT. Use various research methods to gather customer feedback and insights, including surveys, interviews, focus groups, and "managing by walking around." Guide the group in analyzing the data and identifying key consumer expectations. Remember, customers and users are not the same!

Develop QoE and QoS specification pairs.

Develop quality of experience specifications based on the consumer expectations identified in Step 1. First, capture QoE RATER requirements, metrics, and targets. Next, develop the paired QoS operational metrics and quality of experience requirements to deliver and track QoE. A spreadsheet works well for this tracking. Expect a lively discussion about the trade-offs between QoE and QoS resource constraints!

Assign responsibility for implementing each solution to specific individuals or teams. Ensure they have the necessary resources, support, and authority to perform their duties.

Position delivery in the Zone of Tolerance.

Based on the workshop results, prioritize the gaps. Use the QoS/QoE pairing to understand what to resolve. Focus on those gaps that impact digital employee experience and IT satisfaction most or can be addressed with the least effort.

Communicate with consumers and IT staff.

Create a communication plan that informs customers and users about the changes on the way. You should have business and user community representatives as part of creating and sharing this plan.

They can help deliver the news to the front lines, perhaps better than you could. Identify the key communication channels, messages, frequency, and messenger. Focus on the importance of transparency and honesty in your joint communications.

Share the plan and progress toward the goals with all stakeholders, including customers, employees, and leadership. Engage them in the process and seek their feedback and suggestions for improvement.

Review operational technology.

Analyze the root causes of the gaps to determine why they exist. It may be helpful to conduct further research or analysis to understand the underlying issues. This will help to ensure that the action plan addresses the root causes and not just the symptoms of the problem.

Capture every point of control over digital employee experience for a given IT solution.

The controls you want to find and consider must relate to one or more of the five RATER determinates. List every technical attribute of your solution that you can think of — ask, "What controls do we have over the user's experience?"

Don't try to decide if it would add value or not. Write down every single item you have control over which affects the Reliability, Assurance, Tangibles, Empathy, or Responsiveness of this IT solution. It might even seem like it wouldn't please users, but write it down — remember my IBM story?

Consider all the standard IT metrics like throughput, latency (used by the IBM engineers), various capacities, etc. All the usual suspects. And then keep going. For example, technical support, escalations, "white glove" or executive services, standby and spares, backup systems, etc.

Think about the things you don't usually think about, like sales quotas, marketing plans, manufacturing tolerances, seasonal and other intensifiers. Getting to know your internal customers and users can make things evident that you would've never thought to check. Think about the Liberty Mutual example again. They changed the IT maintenance window to accommodate external and customer preferences. They would have never known if they hadn't spent time talking to contact personnel.

Avoid conversations around whether something is positive or negative. If you have control over it, add it to the list. Save the dialogue, monologue, argument, and tit-for-tat for some other time.

Work as a team, stay open-minded, and focus on the prize!

Once you find a potential source of dissatisfaction, you've got something you can work with. It's more than likely that what you've uncovered is something that you can control too. And when you do, IT satisfaction will increase because you've decreased digital friction and allowed your users to get their job done and customers to meet their business commitments, and that's what we're trying to do, right?

Be careful to complete a full study, and don't stop as soon as you find one thing wrong. For example, if you found a Tangibles problem, that might be only around 11% of the total satisfaction or dissatisfaction.

But if you had Empathy and Responsiveness show up as a problem, for example, you'd want to focus on Responsiveness first, and if you do, you're showing Empathy! That's where you'll get the most return on your improvement investment. If you get determinants that are close together, and you're unsure which one to choose, then there is an exercise you can do. Essentially you do a little workshop with those users and have them allocate 100 points across the five RATER determinants. That way, you'll know how they value each determinant. Again, take care because that will only be valuable for that collection of users.

Remember to avoid getting tripped up by the pitfall of focusing only on technology. In many cases, the solution to your IT satisfaction problem has little to do with technology and everything to do with something you never even thought could matter. When you're in the business of improving IT satisfaction, it pays to keep an open mind.

Once you identify the root causes, develop specific solutions to address the gaps. This may involve changes to processes, systems, or people. Consider each solution's feasibility, cost, and impact (BVaR) before deciding which to implement.

Monitor delivery and performance.

Design a service monitoring system to track the solutions' performance against the developed quality specifications. Guide your team using a checklist to identify the key service quality dimensions, metrics, and data sources. Guide them in discussing the challenges of implementing the monitoring system.

Monitor progress towards the goals and adjust the action plan as needed. Continuously evaluate the effectiveness of the solutions and make changes if necessary. Following these steps, you can develop an action plan to close the gaps and improve user experience, which shows higher IT satisfaction. Always remember that IT satisfaction is a lagging indicator.

Measure QoE, and repeat.

Build a customer satisfaction survey to measure the gaps between customer and user expectations and perceptions of the solution delivery (those are different groups with unique surveys!)

Use a satisfaction team to identify key experience dimensions and metrics. Guide the group in discussing the challenges of collecting and analyzing IT satisfaction data.

Set specific goals and metrics to measure progress toward closing the gaps. This will help to track progress and identify when additional actions may be needed.

After every significant change and before any planned changes that can affect QoE, reconvene your IT satisfaction team. Making any substantive change in IT can often induce unexpected consequences in experience. This is something seldom considered by the IT Change Management process, as that process is often more about the technical and operational functionality vs. maintaining the desired experience levels.

The workflow covered in this chapter is illustrative — a great example, but not a stringent outline to maniacally follow. Adapt it, improvise, and you'll soon overcome your IT dissatisfaction.

CONCLUSION

When I started working in technology, user experience was simple, but that's not how things are anymore!

When I entered the workforce, an MIS solution (what we called IT before the name "IT" came into use!) either worked or didn't. My users were highly trained experts who appreciated the time savings, consistency, and productivity enhancement of what we delivered.

Little by little, as technology democratized and commoditized and every business function became reliant upon IT, I realized that we were creating evermore complex solutions and that we'd reached a tipping point. IT solutions were starting to impede productivity. Customers and users were no longer delighted with our IT work.

I went back to school to study the phenomenon, gained a Ph.D., and since then have focused on digital employee experience — increasing employee engagement and productivity by helping IT leaders and their teams improve satisfaction by removing digital friction. I've learned what works and what doesn't and developed my skills at diagnosing and correcting IT solutions and functions to deliver business agility by focusing on digital employee experience and cost-effectiveness with IT satisfaction as my guide.

You can too! You've read this book, which positions you better than I was when I started. More importantly, you have a competitive advantage over your peers and competitors. You now have a proven 10-step process for diagnosing any experience problem, including three IT satisfaction styles you can use for any IT or business product, service, or solution.

Now, all you need to do is take action. I recommend that you reflect on the following points:

- **Any IT product, service, or solution, whether premise, cloud, or hybrid, can completely satisfy its consumers.** How do your consumers feel about your delivery? Do you know what experience your consumers want and need? Your IT solutions can improve, and you can do it right now without buying more technology, hiring expensive, disruptive consultant firms, or waiting for the next escalation.
- **Great digital employee experience comes from leading with satisfaction, nothing else.** What is the range of acceptable performance for your digital employees? What quality of experience do you provide? To improve DEX, engagement, productivity, and profits, you must make digital employee experience your north star, your compass. Lead with it!
- **Seeking out the dissatisfied, learning what they cannot accomplish, and why that matters to your company will always show you where and how to improve satisfaction.** How will you link business agility and profits to your IT strategy? Can you describe how users of your CRM, ERP, SCM, BI, HRM, BA, Fraud Prevention, or manufacturing applications feel about those apps? Do you truly understand the people the users of your business systems work with and the activities they perform?

- **Every IT problem you face comes from Gaps 1, 2, 3, or 4.**
  It's truly that simple — and precisely that complicated.
  Where do your missed expectations in delivery come from?
  Find out and start there!

There is a significant difference between knowing how to do something and leading others to gain similar capabilities. It's easy to execute once you've attained the "muscle memory" to do so. It's less easy to capture what you know instinctively and use it to teach others how to function at the same level.

I have dedicated decades of study and work to simplify one of the most ambiguous and complex activities faced by many IT leaders, both presently and in the future. I've condensed this process into ten steps based on five core concepts and two structures.

My goal is nothing less than to give you the missing link to solving a nagging problem that has bothered you for years — how to lead with satisfaction to nail its delivery for better digital employee experience, productivity, and profits.

Some closing thoughts for your personal and professional success.

Business agility is the term that explains the benefits of leading with IT satisfaction and being experience-centric today. The added nuance is taking action. Now.

To drive business agility, we must be efficient, market aware, proactive, and adaptive, provide a quality experience, be innovative, and learn to co-create.

As IT leaders, I've shown you how we can play a critical role in helping our firms achieve these emerging business goals. Here are seven characteristics you can cultivate to help your business increase its agility:

1. **Efficiency**: Streamlining IT processes, removing digital friction, reducing costs, and improving employee efficiency and productivity.
2. **Market awareness:** Keeping close to digital employees and the external customers they support.
3. **Proactivity**: Spotting employee trends and adjusting operations and offerings accordingly.
4. **Adaptability**: Adjusting to changing employee needs, industry trends, and market conditions.
5. **Quality of experience**: Consistently managing toward improved digital employee experience by keeping deliver in the ZoT.
6. **Innovation**: Staying ahead of your competition by doing what they haven't figured out yet.
7. **Prosumer-focused**: Understanding the wants and needs of those you serve and co-creating IT solutions that meet them.

Coincidently — or perhaps not — a focus on digital employees and improving their digital employee experience reflects the above seven qualities.

IT satisfaction and profits (business agility!) will follow if your goal is reducing digital friction to improve your employee experience. But here's the key to success: You must deliberately decide to achieve these goals by leading with satisfaction. Only by being purposeful, honest, and empathetically engaged with your employees and customers can you spot options that lead to better, more informed decisions.

Good luck, and stay in touch by connecting with me on www.hankmarquis.com or LinkedIn.

ABOUT THE AUTHOR

Hank Marquis is a globally recognized Information Technology entrepreneur, leader, executive advisor, and author with over 30 years of experience in IT.

For the last 20 years, Hank has specialized in simplifying complex IT solutions and enabling technology leaders to excel in digital employee experience and IT leadership.

With a Ph.D. in organizational leadership and multiple IT and quality certifications, Hank combines scholarly insight with practical strategies to transform businesses — he keeps things lite, though, and calls himself an IT Satisfactioneer, and what he does IT Satisfactioneering.

As a popular speaker, he delivers keynotes and sessions at numerous events. Hank has founded startups, authored books, contributed to international best practices, and guided countless individuals and companies to success.

He serves C-level leadership and their direct reports through assessment, workshops, keynotes, and executive advisory services.

See hankmarquis.com and connect with Hank on LinkedIn.

Visit www.hankmarquis.com for free templates and expanded content.

Don't miss out!

Visit the website below and you can sign up to receive emails whenever Hank Marquis publishes a new book. There's no charge and no obligation.

https://books2read.com/r/B-A-LIPX-WZMJC

Connecting independent readers to independent writers.

About the Author

Dr. Henry A. ("Hank") Marquis, Ph.D., FBCS CITP, is an executive advisor, coach, speaker, and author who helps technology leaders simplify complex IT solutions for digital employees. He is a globally recognized IT digital employee experience and service management expert. He has launched five startups and helped countless IT leaders across his thirty-plus-year career as CEO and CTO. Through assessment, workshops, keynotes, and advisory services, Hank advises leadership, IT, HR, and customer success teams.

www.hankmarquis.com

Read more at https://www.hankmarquis.com.

www.ingramcontent.com/pod-product-compliance
Lightning Source LLC
Chambersburg PA
CBHW051311130726
47987CB00004B/1747